StOLeN CHiLD

StOLeN CHiLD
StOLeN CHiLD

Denny
Best Wishes,
Karen

Stolen Child
Stolen Child
Stolen Child

What would you do
if the government stole
your six year old child?

KAREN NOLAN

BLUE NOTE BOOKS
FLORIDA

Published by Blue Note Books, Florida
1-800-624-0401
www.BlueNoteBooks.com

Library of Congress Control Number: 2010911477

ISBN-10: 1-878398-31-8
ISBN-13: 978-1-878398-31-4

First U.S. Edition 2010

Cover Design: Paul Maluccio
Book Interior Design: Petra Micova

Printed in the United States of America

"POWER IS RESPONSIBILITY; IT IS SERVICE, NOT PRIVILEGE. ITS EXERCISE IS MORALLY JUSTIFIABLE WHEN IT IS USED FOR GOOD OF ALL, WHEN IT IS SENSITIVE TO THE NEEDS OF THE POOR AND DEFENSELESS."

- Pope John Paul II, 1999

DEDICATION

To my "LITTLE MAN", Jamie, my son who has returned,
I LOVE YOU.

To THE MANY PEOPLE WHO NEVER GAVE UP even
in my darkest hours, I thank you. To RONNIE,
my husband and Jamie's father, who now resides
with our Father in Heaven, you were my rock and you
never gave up on our fight. To MISTY, my best friend
and confidant who is also in Heaven, I love and miss
you. Your support throughout this journey cannot go
unrecognized. To my daughters, LISA AND GINA, you
were devastated at the loss of your brother, yet he grew
up with you in your innocent minds. You were my source
of continued strength, not only to overcome drugs and
addiction, but to help me face the years of raising you
to become wonderful polished mothers that you are.
DENYS, my best friend, who never worried about telling
me the truth!

To my now soul mate, Jim, who has put up with my long hours at the computer ticking away at the keys and all the while saying, "keep going baby, you're almost there..." You held my hand; you cried with me, you held me when the pain of remembering was so horrible I wanted to stop, but your love allowed me to continue writing. Thank you for loving me in spite of my constant bad moods while writing this book!

To Dr. Dale Wickstrom-Hill who showed me what courage really looks like. You understand struggles and showed me that through diversity one can succeed. Last but not least to Monsignor (Father) John Caulfield of St. Joseph's Catholic Church in Lakeland, Florida. You were my shoulder; I cannot count the many hours I spent in your office on my knees praying with you for peace in my heart and soul. I found that peace as you know with the personal visit from our Holy Mother as she carried the hate away with Her. You didn't laugh at me when I sat in your office the morning after her visit to me and told you her words just before she took the hate away and giving me Her loving peace, "Be angry, do not hate. They crucified my Son. I was angry, but it is not right to hate. Hate only destroys self, not those that destroy."

Thank you!

ACKNOWLEDGEMENT

First and foremost, I want to thank GOD for creating me and my deep love of children; teaching me humility, patience and endurance.

My Sister, DENISE WILSON who loves me unconditionally, no matter what endeavor I took on or subjected her to.

MY MOTHER who is in heaven, I thank you for the love only a mother could give.

To others for their love and belief in me:

DENYS ANDERSON, JACK MARSHALL, MARY ANN ELLSWORTH, NANCY BLANCHARD, JANICE EMERY, CARI GOMEZ, MIKE FARRELL, JEANNINE AND LARRY BROOME, BARBARA ROBINSON, LESLIE AND DON SMITH. Thank you to all my FRIENDS AT ST. JOSEPH'S

CATHOLIC CHURCH in Lakeland, Florida as well as OUR SAVIOR'S CATHOLIC CHURCH, Cocoa Beach, Florida.

And special thank you to my publisher, PAUL MALUCCIO and his assistant, PETRA MICOVA. Thank you for the confidence, constant accessibility and above all your belief in my book.

"WE MUST ALL WORK FOR A WORLD IN WHICH NO CHILD WILL BE DEPRIVED OF PEACE AND SECURITY, OF A STABLE FAMILY LIFE, OF THE RIGHT TO GROW UP WITHOUT FEAR AND ANXIETY. "

Pope John Paul, II

CONTENTS

PREFACE

N O ONE, ESPECIALLY ME, ever imagined that I
would be writing a book or even contemplating
the crazy idea of putting words down on paper
for anyone and everyone to read! Many years ago, I
wrote a children's book while in college and to this date,
it remains in a folder in the back of my file cabinet. I
always wondered, "Who would read it anyway," or "It is
just a silly little book from my imagination that wouldn't
inspire children to be creative." I am going forth with the
children's book because now I can better understand how
a child's mind works.

Today, and for the past year and a half, I am venturing
into a world that is definitely outside of my comfort zone,
you might say. I am writing a true-life experience, which
at first, was just a painful experience. One I had wished I
could forget, or at least bury deep within my subconscious

so I wouldn't have to deal with it. Then a friend said to me, "Write it down, every sordid little detail so others can learn from your experience or share what you have dealt with. Maybe there is someone out there who has experienced the same event and needs your help to move forward." Someone else with the same experience? No way, that can't be possible! But yet, what if … what if someone else had experienced this same event, this same horror or similar destruction of heart and family that I had? Could my story possibly help?

My answer came from God above, maybe not out loud in a deep male thundering voice, but in a subtle way (from many others). "Yes, it can help in more ways than you know." I have listened to this statement from friends, counselors, priests, my children, and many others who know my story.

Beginning the book was painful, taking six months to write the first chapter, then another three for the second. Now it flows from me, taking moments for tears and prayer to get through the next few lines. Thoughts fly through the air like projectiles, so fast that I have difficulty keeping up or grabbing them deftly enough to put down on paper. I am nearly completed now and my excitement increases as I approach the time when you will read this book.

Am I afraid? Yes, to say the least. I am also excited beyond words and, who knows, maybe by the time you are reading this, I have taken out my forgotten children's book, which was placed in the back of my filing cabinet. I remember reading a quote from Mahatma Gandhi, "You may never know what results may come from your action, but if you do nothing, there will be no result." Thank you God and Mr. Gandhi. Without either of you, this book would not be a reality.

I hope as you read this, you take away with you the knowledge that not everyone can be trusted, especially with our children. I pray that your mind is open and your heart is strong to fight for your own children, your neighbor, or anyone else you know who may have dealings with this agency; one that was created to help people.

This is a true story, and because of pending litigation, as well as protecting the innocent, some of the names have been changed to allow the truth to be told in its entirety.

GOD BLESS YOU AND KEEP YOU
AND YOUR FAMILY SAFE.

Karen

CHAPTER 1

DISCOVERY

THE DEATH OF MY MOTHER, Eunice LaDonna Harris, had a profound affect on my life. From the grave she caused a string of events that brought me to find my son who I believed to be dead for 23 years.

It had been a traumatic day in the operating room from the onset; a patient wasn't doing well, (critical condition with the same illness as my mother's). I sat down to eat dinner and another employee had laid the newspaper of the day, July 11, 2002 on the table. I glanced over and noticed a story about a young two-year-old boy who had been kidnapped and not found. I always made a habit of not reading about those things, not watching news reports or even any kind of movie that remotely resembled that situation. I totally lost all sense of calm and started sobbing, desperately needing to go home.

On the way home, (a 30 minute drive), I plugged in a music CD as I always did, because I rarely ever listened to the radio. The radio invariably had bad news and I couldn't stand to listen to anything going on in the world. The soft beautiful voice of Celine Dion filled the cab of my truck, triggering strong emotions that had been held in way too long. I began to cry so much that I was a mess and unable to see through my tears. I pulled over to the side of the darkened, dreary road and literally punched the CD player to turn it off. I rested my head on the steering wheel and prayed, specifically saying, "Mom, I know you can hear me and I miss you so much. Now that you're in heaven, I need you to please let me know if Jamie's safely with you. If he's not, please, please show me where he is. I can't take it anymore. If he is in Heaven with you, let him know that I love him and miss him beyond words." My sobbing was almost uncontrollable, but then as if a wind blew in the truck, I felt this warm strange calmness overtake my entire body. I knew Mom was listening to me because I was sure I was feeling her arms wrapped around my body. I began to dry my eyes and turned the radio back on. When I did, I bumped the knob and began listening to an unfamiliar radio station, one that I had never heard before with someone named Delilah. Delilah was talking to a woman who profusely thanked her for helping find her long lost daughter through Adoption.com. I thought to myself, "Self don't touch that dial!" I listened long to their conversation as though I was meant to hear it. The woman told her that through Adoption.com, she found her long lost daughter and it had been totally free. The sight tries to extract money for guaranteed results but she claimed, "you just go back, remove information until what you are seeking comes to light".

I thought, "I have gone there just in the hopes that Jamie would be alive and paid many dollars too many times just praying for an answer, yet found nothing." Mom wanted me to hear this again, so I listened. Again I thought, "This is my answer. I need to do as this woman did."

With my eyes dried and my composure revived, I took off down the road, heading home. On arrival, I immediately headed towards the computer in the office. My husband was sound asleep so I started my detailed search at 10:45 pm. At 12:55 am, the keys were starting to blur, my eyes were burning, and I was exhausted, but I was so close I couldn't give up. I had three names ... three matches, actually four, but one was a girl. The excitement was escalating; I was beside myself ... down to two and ... "Oh ... My ... God!"

CHAPTER 2 _____

A LONG DELIVERY

PREGNANCY, THAT FLUFFY ENORMOUS bloated feeling where you no longer feel your nose or see your feet, experience! Nine months of happy torture. Who ever said that it was wonderful was only half right. They must have been in a dream like state of drug induced euphoria or had a pregnancy with no complications, no swelling, a tiny six pound baby, and a three hour labor with only ten minutes of pushing. My pregnancy for Jamie really wasn't all that tragic. I vomited the first three months steady and waddled like a duck the rest. I could sit on the couch and place a plate flat on my tummy to eat a meal. My girth measured 49" around (and I started with 19"). Mom found it rather cute. My younger sister, Kathy, used to be amused by it, especially the day my young "offspring" decided my plate must have been too warm and sent it flying to the floor with a swift "soft" punch or kick. Then of course, I could not bend over to clean it up. My mother and sister laughed a great deal over that one yet neither of them tried to help as I, with great difficulty, attempted to clean things up. They just continued to laugh and laugh. To the point of tears, I might add! Even in utero, Jamie was causing quite a ruckus!

His entry into this world was as comical and adventurous as well. Mom and I went out to the "Saints and Sinners" lounge in Altamonte Springs. I told her that I was becoming too "house-bound" and needed a night out. We listened to music and talked to people for much of the evening. I even had a young gentleman come and ask me to dance, until I turned around and he realized I was "very" pregnant. From the rear, it was obvious to no one that I carried a *huge* belly with child! While sitting at the bar, I tapped my mom on the shoulder very gently and whispered in her ear, "I think my water is leaking, something feels strange." At this point, I was two weeks past my due date and it was Tuesday, November 12, 1974, 11:45pm. My mother, who was always the calmest in any given situation, yelled, "Is there a doctor here, my daughter's water has broken!" The bartender, whose name was Jamie, started to panic and shoved glasses of several types of liquid at me, 7 UP, orange juice, cranberry juice, water, etc. I laughed and said, "I don't think they will make any difference, but thank you anyway!" Mom and I left with me in the driver's seat—imagine that. She had taken in too much to drink and I was really feeling fine. I had no cramps, pains or any of those horrible things I had seen on television where the woman grabs her abdomen and starts having a baby right there! I kept waiting for that moment, but we got home without further incident. The leakage must have only been urine from another one of his adventurous kicks and I went to bed around 1:00 am.

Somewhere around 1:30 am, I began to feel a little uncomfortable as if someone had wrapped a vice around me. I was squeezed so hard that I could not breathe. It eased up for a few minutes and was followed by gas pains, of all things, until a few minutes later, when it started happening again, and again. By now, I was thinking this must be something to be concerned about, so I went to wake up mom who was still intoxicated and not easily aroused. However, she managed to say to me, "Go ahead honey, the keys are on the table."

I thought for a second, "Well—I did drive home earlier. OK, this should be fine and I'm not going that far. I can do this, she can't drive and no one else is here." So off I went to the hospital ten miles away. In my nightgown, robe, and sneakers, a true fashion statement, I took off in my mother's huge white Cadillac Coupe Deville convertible. About five miles down the road, a really big contraction hit me like someone tied an anchor to my lungs and tried to yank them out from my abdomen or lower. I pulled off to the side of the road with the back end of the car still hanging out in the driving lane, unbeknownst to me. Resting my head on my hands over the wheel I felt that there must be something wrong. I was sweating, could hardly breathe, and it felt like someone was ripping my belly open. "God, I must be dying!" At this precise moment, I saw bright red flashing lights and I thought; ok, now I am dying.

Within seconds of the bright lights, I realized I was not dying. I heard this 'tap-tap-tap' on the window and noticed it was a policeman. Thank you God for sending me help! I used the wonderful invention of the electric button for the window, thank you to whoever invented it, and I heard this stern voice say to me, "You got a problem Lady, too much to drink?" I sat straight up as the pain had subsided. All sweaty, pale faced, and dressed only in a robe, I whispered, "No, my mother had too much to drink and I am in labor." The police officer forgot he was supposed to be in an irritated state and I am not sure if he was about to pass out or if I was, but abruptly he jutted his arm in the forward motion of the hospital direction, and yelled, "follow me". I didn't really expect that answer, but I was young, swollen like a whale, and in pain, so I put the car in gear and headed in behind him. Now, either it was my naïve state or just dumb luck, but we made it the next few miles into the front of the hospital. He got me a wheelchair, a nurse, who took the keys, and we departed to some unknown busy, noisy place. I never did get the officer's name, but I do know that he remained there long enough to park the car and find out if I was ok. I think back on it now and wonder if the police would be so gallant today, or would they just call an ambulance and leave? Maybe we both were naïve! Throughout all of this, remember my mother was still at home with no real sense of awareness. She was still in bed, oblivious to the fact that I had driven to the hospital in labor at two o'clock in the morning, with her car.

My obstetrician, whose choice of profession baffles me even now, was in another hospital delivering twins and for some reason the nurses who were attending me, lead him to believe I was very close to delivery. He had them transfer me to where he was … in another town 30 miles away.

My mother woke up around 8 am to find me, and her car gone. She began to panic as the fog was beginning to lift and she remembered bits and pieces of our 1:30 am conversation, if you can call it that. She hysterically called the neighbor to inform her of the huge fiasco that was going on and they started off for the hospital. Mom arrived at the Apopka hospital, finding her car but no me. They informed her of the transfer and handed her the keys. This was early Wednesday afternoon, November 13, 1974. She finally arrived expecting to find a new grandchild, her first, and only found me still in labor and not at all happy. They were giving me pitosin nose drops (do they even have those anymore?) every 15 minutes to induce "stronger" labor pains! Now I know anyone who has endured labor pains knows that stronger means to land a semi tractor trailer on top of your chest for approximately three to four minutes. Why on earth did anyone want to make it a front-end loader stuffed with concrete blocks, I will never know!

She sat with me and we talked about everything from her experiences to who knows what else. The day went on forever and around nine in the evening, the doctor stated that I was only dilated to five and the nurse told me that first babies take longer. I was not having a lot of pain, just extremely aggravated. Mom decided to go rest in the lobby and I slept the rest of the night. I don't know how but it was as if the labor just stopped. Thursday morning, around 11 am, Dr. M walked in and decided to increase the medicine in my nose drops, saying, "We need to speed things up for you and the baby." What is he, some sort of masochist? I started having some horrendous contractions just knowing the child had no intention of coming out of there. He had decided to stay forever! My Lord, I feel as if the child is hanging on to my ribcage and truly had no intention of exiting the warm place in which he has become accustomed! At 4 pm, the doc came in to inspect the progress, if you can call it that, all while in contraction. It hurts like I have not only endured a crane entering me, but I have someone's huge yeti hands measuring my progress. Did I take it like a lady, heck no! I nailed him with a perfect left hook and he turned to leave. At this, I have had enough. I got up, ripped everything off me and started walking down the hall, butt hanging out and barely dressed. "That's it, I'm done, and I'm not doing this." My backside is now really hanging out, gown flapping in the wind behind me. "I'm leaving … Mom get me…" and then the big one hit again, this horrendous, horrific, air depleting contraction that started ripping me in half! Two nurses grabbed me under each arm and literally dragged me back to my "cell" to hook me back up. The next few hours were like being on a terrifyingly awful roller coaster. Then I remember lots of drugs, the doctor having me sign a paper because the baby was just too big and I was going to sleep … deeply to sleep.

I awoke to the most beautiful sight I had ever seen. My mother was smiling down at this little dark haired baby, all wrapped up in a soft white with blue trim blanket. I could barely speak. She looked up at me and I softly said, "What did I have?"

"A Boy."

"How much does he weigh?"

"Seven pounds, nine ounces."

With barely a whisper, I asked her, "How long is he?"

"Twenty-one inches long."

Then from out of the stellar space and for some unknown reason to anyone or myself I vividly remember saying, "I feel the intrusion of the Gentlemen's gambling." I have no idea what this means or why I said it, but I did.

My mother burst out laughing and woke my new son—his lungs were in perfect condition I recall. I reached for him, yet I was so weak she carried him to me, placed him in my arms, and guided him to my left breast. He acted like he was never going to get food again and I felt that the child was camped on that breast for life! The nurses were in love with him and every time they brought him to me, they would fawn all over him telling me how ebony dark and beautiful his hair and eyes were. His beautiful skin, so olive in color, looked as if he had already been tanned by the sun. One nurse came in the next morning to find me maintaining him totally unwrapped, him sucking on the breast, again like he would never get it back, kissing each and every finger and toe.

"Oh my," she clamored, "you must keep him covered, he will catch his death from exposure." I told her that I was just examining his perfectness and loved to smell, admire, and kiss him.

Naming him was easy—Jamie, because I loved the sound of the name of the panicked bartender who wanted to force fluids on me, and William, after my grandfather. They would have the same initials as we planned on calling him J.W., which Grandpa had been so affectionately called, but it never happened.

Mom and I brought him home after five days (imagine staying that long now) and he wrapped himself around everyone's hearts. Those big beautiful sable brown eyes melted the hearts of every person who dared to peer into them. His Aunt Kathy had only to walk by when he would make the slightest squeak and she was his for the taking. Jamie molded everyone to his routine instead of the other way around. Aunt Kathy bought him a stuffed monkey, which became a part of him, like a blanket. It went everywhere with him and they were never apart. I had to wash it when he was sleeping or the screaming would go on for hours. It was easier to sneak it out from under his armpit during the night, which in itself was not an easy feat since he was a not a deep sleeper, but I would gingerly manage to get it out, wash it, and return it, before the monkey was ever missed!

CHAPTER 3

EARLY TALENTS

DAYS, MONTHS, AND YEARS PASSED quickly by. Jamie spoke early, walked quickly … ever too quickly … and was into everything all the time. He was the smartest "little person" I had ever encountered.

At two years old, we bought Jamie a toy train for Christmas that tooted and the light blinked on and off. He immediately began taking it apart dissecting every trinket he removed, touching and rolling them in his fingers. I almost could not believe my eyes when I saw him put it back together and it worked as if it never had been apart! He did things like that all the time. I thought to myself, "This kid is going to be an engineer or architect." Figuring things out was his goal at hand.

He had a keen sense of awareness and memory. I am not sure what it was or how, but he knew things that even baffled me. He had to be a genius! I had four keys on my key chain, all not that very different, and he could tell me what each one went to, even when I mixed them up or took them off the ring.

One day, about a week later, I decided there was no way he would remember now, so I put the four keys on the table in the kitchen with his daddy sitting there and said, "Jamie, what are these and do you know what they are for?"

He picked each one up, examined it, and went with one of them to put it in the door. Ronnie almost fainted, he said, "Son, do that again, where do the other ones go?"

Jamie carried the other three around, placing two of them at the correct spot, except for one, which belonged to my sister-in-law's house. Jamie just glared at it with frustration, held it up shaking his head and replied, "aon't know." We thought that this was truly a gifted child and we had the smartest little person on earth!

Jamie loved to play outdoors and go for walks. He was fascinated with clouds, birds, trees, and dogs. He loved the wind, loved kisses, hugs, and stories (no matter how many times he heard them) being read to him, and copying Nana's flair for art, especially coloring all over things he wasn't supposed to color on. Examples of these things would be his bed, walls, shoes, television, cars, and thinking on it now, the list is almost endless.

Jamie was definitely set in his ways about clothes he would wear or not wear. (This will be pertinent later on). When he was three and a half years old, I bought him a pair of coveralls; you know the cute little ones like "train conductors" wear. Well, I fought with him for an hour and he would not even put one whole leg in. "These are sissy, no mamma, please give them away ... nooooo!"

I kept telling him, "They're not sissy, men wear them, train conductors wear then, and farmers wear them." But not my son, no way. So, we settled for putting on a pair of jeans and the coveralls were donated to someone or something.

Trouble seemed to start subtly. When I think back on it now, as I write this book, it may even have been as far back as when we moved to my mothers when Jamie was three. I think he didn't want to share me, and my mother spoiled him rotten. Here, he was an only child, living with Grandma and Mommy ... what a sweet deal! He had it made. Anything he wanted, Grandma gave him. In the evening, although our beds were in the same room, I would wake up and find him snuggled up next to me in mine. I moved out of moms a few months after moving in and at that time, I was a single mom.

CHAPTER 4

THE FOUNDATION

I WASN'T LONELY. I dated some, but nothing seemed to stick. My best friend, Misty, and her boyfriend, Jack, kept insisting they needed to fix me up with Jack's brother, Ronnie. I wasn't having any part of that and I continued "warding" them off. Misty and Jack were quite the scheming pair and decided to take matters into their own hands. On Halloween, 1977, Jack conveniently got stuck without a ride home in St. Cloud and Misty was the rescuer. She asked me if I would like to go along for the ride as it was an hour drive and she would love the company, so I said, sure. We arrived at the Horseshoe Bar, walked in and Jack kissed Misty and said, "Hi, Karen, this is my brother, Ronnie." I was furious, yet couldn't admit to them that I was entirely attracted to him. That evening became the "rest of our lives" for me that at that time, yet it lasted only two months. He met Jamie the next day and informed me he wanted to be his father. He told me after just two weeks of dating that he was moving in, that, "Jamie needed a father," and that was that. The two of them were inseparable. Wherever Ronnie went, Jamie was there and he just automatically called him Daddy.

In December of 1977, Ronnie's wife who I had just found out about, decided to stick her head in the oven because she couldn't live without him, and he went "Home to Her"! I was devastated, but not as much as Jamie. His "Daddy" had deserted him, his "Daddy" was gone and he began acting up. Little things at first, temper tantrums in the kitchen when he didn't get his way, or dumping his food on the floor on purpose.

A few weeks after Ronnie left, the temperature outside dropped and I felt as though I was catching the flu. The mornings were getting very cold and my body didn't seem to be able to regulate at all. One morning as I vividly remember, I finally figured out that I was involved, yet again, in the most horrible bout of morning sickness. I looked down the hallway to see my son covered in white soapy bubbles and smelling very clean and fresh. I asked him what he was doing and he proudly proclaimed with this enormous smile, "I washed the fish for you, Mommy!"

Puzzled, I walk into the living room to see the entire fish tank encapsulated in bubbles while all the fish were floating on top. Every morning we experienced another adventure, or should I say, mini disaster. Short of taping the child to the bed, I was beside myself and confided in my mother. She informed me that there was counseling service available for little or no cost, so I called them. This low cost counseling group turned out to be associated with Health and Rehabilitative Services and it most definitely would be free.

We began going weekly with each of us having individual sessions and it helped Jamie for a while. The "strange" episodes of behavior calmed down and things were leaning more towards the happy side. The little boy I loved so much was returning.

CHAPTER 5

THE NEW GIFT

MY PREGNANCY WAS GOING WELL and Jamie started to kiss my belly all the time telling his baby that he couldn't wait for "her" arrival. We were bonding again, just Jamie and I, and the baby in my tummy. Everything was going great until 7 ½ months into the pregnancy, when I was in an auto accident and a drunk driver plowed head into my car. The rescue personnel worked diligently to remove me, but to no avail. They had to call in the "jaws of life" as the steering wheel was imbedded into my abdomen. With the seat pushed all the way back, I couldn't move in any direction. My abdomen began to cramp and pain like I had never known before. It was a searing, immense stretching sensation that was beginning to strip me of all reason.

One pain, and then another until I thought I was dying. I knew my baby was in serious trouble. I started screaming. At first I didn't realize it was me screaming, begging the emergency people to save my baby at all cost. I didn't care about me, but they had to save the baby. The next thing I could remember was being in the hospital in the labor suite with my physician telling me to try and relax.

"They are giving you something to stop the contractions so this little one can stay in there longer, but you have to do your part and think good thoughts."

I promised that I would try and started telling them that Jamie would have to be picked up from preschool soon; someone had to contact my girlfriend. Prayers were coming fast and furious. I begged God to care for the little one in my womb, Jamie's new baby, and help our family.

For the next week, Jamie stayed with Misty and again, he began acting up—screaming, slapping the other children, biting, and not eating. Misty said, "This will calm down, he is just feeling a little abandoned, but when you get home, things will be OK."

I prayed it would. I prayed for my little baby, and I prayed that I would never see Ronnie again! The third day of my hospitalization, Misty called and asked if someone else could come and get Jamie. She herself had a newborn of two weeks at home and her son was the same age as Jamie. She sobbed, "Having the two boys the same age is destroying my composure." Jamie had urinated in her closet, screamed at her constantly, and disobeyed terribly.

He was too much for her to handle and I begged the doctors to let me go home. My mother took him for the next few days and I arrived home on Saturday. Jamie was mad at me; he barely would look at me and just went to his room. The following Monday, I called the counseling center and back we went. This seemed to help, although I am not sure if it was the counseling that helped a little or the fact that I was home.

I was still very pregnant and didn't feel like arguing with a 3-½ year old. I let him do just about anything he wanted to do. For the next two and a half months we went back to our usual routine—breakfast, consisting of cereal or his favorite french toast, school, coming home, reading stories, coloring, and going for walks to Misty's apartment. Her apartment was only three buildings over from ours, and we seemed to be happy again. We attended counseling together and he also went alone. This began working and Jamie again became my sweet "little man", helping me, talking sweetly to me, cuddling my belly, and talking to "his" new baby.

CHAPTER 6

ADVANCEMENT

LISA, OUR NEW BUNDLE OF JOY came into the world rather quickly on August 27, 1978. Jamie at first was thrilled. He watched me change her, breast feed her, and we were a happy family of three. This was his new sister and he adored her. We would always play together and sit and do things while I would nurse her, or he would help me in anyway he could.

Halloween rolled around just after Lisa was three months old and I had taken a bartending job with Misty at her place of work. Misty and I had already hired a wonderful woman by the name of Janet to care for Jamie and her son, Brian. She had been taking care of Jamie for the whole year; so needless to say, she acquired Lisa and Misty's new arrival of six months, Michelle. Here it is

Halloween at this horrible "strip joint" where we worked. Misty was not a stripper, she was the waitress and I the bartender. The place was packed. It could have been the moon, or the mood of the so-called season, but we had never been that busy. I looked up and almost fainted as none other than Ronnie walked in, whom I hadn't seen in eight months, professing his undying love for me and exclaiming with a large grin that he had a present. I just glared and told him and his brother to leave, stating I wanted nothing more to do with him or his so called affection. I never wanted to see or hear from him again. I turned to start filling up icy beer mugs and thought, this is just how I feel about him, "cold and icy!"

I was furious, believing Jack, his brother, and Misty, my supposed best friend, had informed Ronnie of his new daughter. He kept insisting he wasn't leaving until I talked to him. Finally, after hours of him begging me, I agreed to see what he wanted. When the bar had closed, we went to Denny's Restaurant for coffee. Now, mind you it was 2:40 in the morning and I am not only tired but also very irritated and still icy like the beer mugs I had in my possession all evening.

Sitting at the table, there was this awkward moment of familiarity. Here was this man I had been so in love with and still was, but would not let him know that. He had built my son's hope up for a good loving father, and he was the father of my newborn baby girl, yet he left me for the wife I had known nothing about. I wanted to kiss and choke him at the same time, but I decided, "What the heck, we were there and I might as well listen to what he had to say."

I was almost certain he would lay claim to Lisa, letting me know that Jack or Misty had told him. He proceeded to tell me he loved me and handed me his present—his neatly typed up divorce papers. I was shocked and angry because I felt it was all a ruse to get his daughter and me back into his life. He did most of the talking and we left a couple of hours later to bring me home. My rat fink friend, Misty, had my car and was supposed to wait for me, but decided that she was tired and Ronnie could bring me home!

We had to go to Janet's to pick up the children and Ronnie came to carry Jamie down. It was very cold outside, almost as icy as those dang beer mugs I couldn't get out of my mind, and he had left the car on so it would stay warm. While I was gathering up Lisa's diaper bag and Jamie's monkey, I thought to myself, "now why hasn't he returned to help?" He was sitting in the car oblivious to what else was going on, just waiting for me to come down. I called to him telling him I needed further help.

He asked, "What about Jamie in the car, it's running with the heat on?"

I said he would be all right for a couple of minutes. He walked into the apartment and saw Janet holding Lisa and said, "Janet, when did you have another baby?"

It hit me hard and fast that this man didn't have a

clue, Jack and Misty hadn't betrayed my trust. I informed him with tears in my eyes, "Ronnie, that is not Janet's baby, she's your daughter, our daughter."

He was stunned and his eyes filled with tears as he held out his arms and gently took her to him. He looked at me with such love and awe that I melted. I knew I would allow him back into our lives. Thus began our family.

CHAPTER 7

CONFUSION ENSUES

JAMIE WOKE UP TO FIND "DADDY" BACK with Mommy and was beside himself. He jumped into bed with us and he and Ronnie were off again. Pals forever and again inseparable. Wherever Ronnie went, so went Jamie. Sometimes as I think back on it now, he was afraid daddy would leave him again, but when Ronnie went out on the truck for a week at a time, he would call his "shadow son" every night. When Ronnie was home, his "shadow" was doing, or trying to do, everything his daddy did. They played, cleaned, and worked on motorcycles, the one being rebuilt in the middle of my Florida room to be exact. When it was complete and in the garage they remodeled the Florida room together. I felt great joy in my heart watching these two. Dust was flying everywhere.

Jamie, on the second day, had so much tile dust in his hair that he looked like a gray haired little old man.

In January of 1979, I realized we were adding to the family yet again and this began to affect Jamie in the worst way. Not like he acted when I was pregnant for Lisa, but his Daddy was involved here and he was paying a great deal of attention to mommy and her growing tummy, not him. He began to act up again. First with little things like before, then he graduated to me finding him urinating in the closet in his baby sister's room. I startled him as much as he startled me and I truly believed this time he had been sleep walking. Her room was next to the bathroom, and their rooms were half a house away. But a few nights later, I awoke to him sitting in Lisa's crib with a razor, shaving her head. I became terrified that he would hurt her and contacted HRS yet again for counseling. This seemed to help a little until after the birth of his new baby sister, Gina. Everyone would come around to admire and make cooing noises, wanting to hold her. Even daddy was now giving all his attention to the baby. Jamie started acting out more and more as his individual time with Ronnie became less frequent. He was showing more jealousy over the attention the baby was getting. I suppose that in his mind, a lot of negative attention was better than a little bit of good attention.

We continued counseling, but Jamie was now having trouble in school. His classroom was set up in a "Pod" mode where four classes were molded in one very large room. My son was showing a limited attention span and not making progress, so Ronnie and I showed up one day, unannounced, to view the situation. We peeked in the door to observe Jamie's teacher doing arithmetic, while the teacher behind him was reading a story. He, of course, as with several other children, found the story much more entertaining than arithmetic. We observed approximately five children who were turned around in their seats. The teachers claimed this had nothing to do with Jamie's inattentiveness. I, as well as his father, stated that we would rather listen to a story, one that Jamie was enraptured with, than do "work". The Pod classroom system did not survive and it was gone before the end of the year.

Jamie would come home from school and eat like he was ravenous. He loved to play outside and ride his bike, but unfortunately for us and most of St. Cloud, he would wander off. I had to go look for him several times. He had become the town "visitor". Almost everyone within a very short time knew who he was and where he lived. At six years old, he knew the town of St. Cloud, Florida, better than his mother. I even listened as one of the fireman who returned him, exclaimed, "This little guy is quite the challenge, isn't he? He sure knows where to come and get goodies."

I thanked him profusely and told him I wished he would never have to return him again, but we both knew that wouldn't be true. He laughed and tousled Jamie's chocolate brown hair, telling Jamie to stay out of trouble, and left. I knew I would probably be seeing him again, with that son of mine always wandering off. My biggest fear was that he would wander off and someone would abduct or hurt him. The problem was, Jamie wasn't afraid of anything or anyone.

The family seemed to be settling pretty well. Gina was four months old and Ronnie and I discussed the fact that more children would be a burden on our finances. We talked about several things and he stated flatly, "Having a knife in the area of his favorite possession was totally out of the question!" Him wearing a form of "rain coat" wasn't an option either and since we were the fertility couple of the decade, meaning that the girls are 11 months and 12 days apart, we couldn't leave things to chance.

One of the things I became certain of is that the statement, "You cannot conceive a child while breastfeeding", is a myth. I was thinking that we were certainly safe since I was at the time, breastfeeding Lisa. Abstinence, of course, was totally out of the question, so our only option was a tubal ligation. Ronnie went with me for my six-month check up where we sat with the doctor to discuss our options. Again, I repeat, all the previous ideas were no longer on the table for discussion. The doctor told us it was a relatively simple procedure. A small incision was made about an inch long and I would go home from the hospital the next day. That didn't sound too awful for me, so I allowed the doctor to schedule it for April 15, 1980. Gina was "sort of" taking breast milk out of a bottle and since he said the word "simple", one day, home the next, I agreed it would be okay. I told him that I still needed to make sure in my heart because I was a Catholic and it was something "forbidden by the church".

Away from the doctor's office we went and Ronnie was overjoyed a "fix" had been scheduled and it definitely did not involve him or his "family" member! The next month confirmed it for me as I somehow caught the flu. For two days straight I vomited and my first thought was, "Oh my God, I'm pregnant again." I quickly called the doctor. He had told me that the flu was going around, but I wanted to have a pregnancy test done anyway. A couple of days later I was informed it was indeed negative and I confirmed my surgery date with his nurse. My mother in law, Sister in law, Janice, and Misty informed us they would help with the children, so we were all set.

April 14th arrived and Ronnie and I drove to the hospital to check in the night before. As we kissed all the little ones goodbye at Janice's door, I had a nagging doubt whether we were doing the right thing. Janice told me later that week that Mom took over the very next morning with the children after our son decided to sit in front of her fan and cut his hair on her newly waxed floor! She was fit to be tied and unfortunately, at the time, I kind of giggled. Not to her actually, but all I could picture was his black hair which was kind of long, flying through the air all over her newly waxed kitchen floor. It must have been a surreal event!!

Back at the hospital, surgery day was here and I swore from then on, I would not return to the Catholic Church. A greenhorn, cocky, young priest came in to my hospital room just before they were to take me to the operating room. He proceeded to tell me that I was committing a mortal sin by sterilizing myself. I felt sick in my stomach and told Ronnie, but we both knew we could not afford any more children. I was full of guilt and shaking when they took me into the operating room suite. It was the best decision of my life because had I not gone through with it, they never would have found the ovarian cancer tucked behind my uterus and filling up my right ovary.

I woke up with this huge bandage across my abdomen, which should have only been band-aid size. Ronnie told me they came to him in the waiting room and had him sign the consent to remove all my female organs. He was so sorry, but said they told him it was my only chance to live. I was upset to say the least; back then ... young, dumb and blonde me ... assumed I would now grow a beard and wouldn't be a "woman" anymore.

The doctor assured me that wasn't the case and he would put me on hormones to replace the ones I wouldn't manufacture anymore. He then informed me I needed to start Chemo right away. My youthful ignorance kicked into gear informing them I was still breast feeding the eight month old daughter he delivered and it would have to wait until she was weaned. The only understanding I had of Chemotherapy at that time was that everything new being produced in your body stopped abruptly ... and I couldn't have the breast milk stop. I told the doctor that I would call as soon as Gina was weaned, and we went home.

In June of 1980, I received a phone call from the police department to tell me that Jamie and his dog, Boof, were on the roof of a restaurant. I nearly fainted and ran over there, which was only a block away from the house, to see them both proudly, mind you, staring at me with a grin from ear to ear. I swear even Boof was grinning. I could not believe my eyes and neither did the police, restaurant owner or townspeople. No one could figure out how he even got himself, let alone a dog, up on the roof.

The rest of the week was uneventful until Saturday morning. I got up early to the smell of sulfur and matches burning. I ran to the smell and at that very moment, watched Jamie burning his baby sister's fingers as she stood up in her crib. I screamed at him and at Ronnie to come and get him while I tended to Gina. The burns were very slight, but burns just the same.

After that incident, I went to the phone to call his counselor and she stated we should set up an appointment for extensive testing along with counseling. I agreed.

On August 5th, I started Chemotherapy. It was the most awful gut wrenching stinking experience I've ever gone through. At first, you just lay there while they pump this stuff into your very large vein. Not so bad, but they kept me for two days because after an hour, I felt as if I were vomiting from my feet. I felt that all my innards most definitely had to be in the toilet and I felt like I was dying. I said, "I will not do this again." One treatment was all I was going through and the nurses told me that it gets easier. They gave me some sort of anti-vomiting medicine and it barely took the horrible edge off.

Then they told me that I should cut my almost waist-length blonde hair, because I could "possibly" lose it and it would be less traumatic! I refused that notion and figured that after having to be that sick, I would be relieved of the hair loss concept. WRONG. After my third treatment five days later, I was in the shower and screamed. Ronnie came running in and said, "What, what is it baby?"

I was in full sobs and showed him this long clump of hair in my hand. Ronnie climbed into the shower with me and held me as I sobbed, water still running. He helped dry me off when we got out and he cut my hair for me.

The next two months seemed to go along with a lot of chemo, Jamie being mad at me for being so sick and Daddy busy with his sisters and having little time for him. Jamie became the most "missing" child I had even known. We were constantly going around St. Cloud because he had gone out to play yet again and disappeared. I knew he was upset and I knew that he needed help, but counseling sessions became slim to none due to my illness.

CHAPTER **8**

OPPRESSION

IN THE LAST WEEK of August, 1980, Jamie's counselor advised me that he needed to go visit the Florida Boy's Ranch for an extensive work up and psychological evaluation. She claimed it would really benefit him and it would be for approximately a week while a psychiatrist determined whether he needed to be on medication or not. I told her I would refuse any type of medication and she stated it would also help with a discipline plan. After much deliberation and prayer, Ronnie and I agreed. I went in to her to talk some more and she said I had to sign a "foster care placement" paper in case of emergency. This would be something signed by me that allowed them to get him medical assistance should he become hurt or ill. It felt wrong. I called Ronnie and he said to do what my heart told me to do. I told her I did not want to sign any papers, but she insisted that it was just in the event he needed emergency medical attention and they could not help him without it, so I agreed and signed one piece of paper. At the top of the paper it stated only, "Foster Care Placement" and nothing more.

I went home that afternoon with great heaviness in my heart. Something felt strange inside me, but I attributed it to exhaustion and wanting nothing more than to help my little boy become my loving "little man" again. When Jamie arrived home from school, I told him he was going on a short adventure, to a special school for about a week and we needed to get some things together. This was on a Monday, September 8, 1980 and they were picking him up on a Wednesday. He picked out clothes, socks, his monkey, which he couldn't sleep without, and asked if he could take some pictures. I said. "Sure, Little Man," and together we made a small booklet of pictures with me, his "daddy", Ronnie, Lisa, Gina, his dog Boof, and him on his bike. Then he asked me if he could take his bike. I told him I would check and that evening we all had a wonderful time. I thought, maybe this will help him, but then I began to doubt my decision. Maybe I was over dramatizing the events leading up to this because he acted so sweet and cuddly, like his old self, that evening. Ronnie said that it was only for a week and then he would be back home in our arms where he belonged.

The next morning, Wednesday at approximately

10:00, a man named Max from HRS came and picked up Jamie. Jamie asked him if he could take his bike and he said, "Sure, let's get it loaded up." My heart sank as I saw them putting his things in the car. Something was nagging me to stop this whole event and take my boy back into the house. I was so torn, but I knew I needed my baby boy to be well and Lisa and Gina safe from further attacks of jealousy. As he started to get into the car, he turned around, gave me a great big hug and kisses and said, "When I come back mommy, I will be your good little boy again!" That day was September 9, 1980 and it would be the last time I would see my little boy alive again.

Two days later, I called the "case worker" Jen, to see how he was doing and she said things were going well. I asked if I could go and see him and she said, "Not right now as it would interfere with the evaluation." It hurt my feelings greatly, but I agreed. She then asked me if I had a record of his shots and I told her I did. I brought his baby book to her on Thursday, September 10, 1980. I kept all of his records in there, illnesses, shots, bumps, bruises, and every little adventure he managed to have. His little life diary, so to speak, was all contained in the little blue book. She asked if she could copy the records and of course, I said yes. When she returned from the copy machine, she stated that the copier was not functioning and could I leave the baby book with her and pick it up the next day. I left it with her and the following day, Friday, I went to pick it up. I was also going to ask if I would be able to pick up Jamie on Wednesday, as that would be a week. The first thing I was told was he would not be able to be picked up at that time because evaluations did not occur on the weekends, they would just observe the child during the first few days. I asked her if the copier had been repaired and she told me yes, so I told her I needed to get his baby book since I was there. She returned a few moments later to tell me she could not find it. It had mysteriously disappeared.

"How could that have happened?" I asked her. I told her it was very important to me and she claimed she didn't know, but would continue to look for it. On Friday the following week, I drove to the Florida Boy's Ranch in South Kissimmee and stated that their exam should be over and I wanted my son. I waited for one and a half hours, when finally a doctor, or whatever he was, came to tell me he needed more time with Jamie. He needed to see what made him "tick". I asked to see him and he said it would be detrimental to Jamie's testing at this point. I couldn't believe seeing his mother could hurt him in any way, but being naive as I was, I left because the doctor "said so" and cried all the way home.

September became October and then November followed with me not being allowed to visit my son. On his birthday, November 14, I drove there with presents and waited for three and a half hours. They told me he was in a session and could not be disturbed, but they would make sure he received the presents and would call me after opening them. I heard nothing from him or them. Thanksgiving arrived; I went back and was refused again. Christmas came around and we went with presents and we waited three hours, refusing to leave. They told me that Jamie was at the psychiatrist's house and wouldn't be back for several hours. I stated I would wait, but they said it wouldn't be possible. I was absolutely furious. In tears, I left the presents and turned to leave as the girls were with Ronnie's mom and we needed to pick them up. As if some sort consolation, the attendant told us that Jamie had been progressing well and I should be happy about that. I told her I wanted a call from him that night, no matter how late it was.

When we got home we told Ronnie's parents what had happened. I was hysterical and they said that it was B.S! "They can't do that! Get that lady here on the phone and tell her you are going to get your son!" I called every day for the next three weeks and never was able to talk to anyone. I left message after message and no one returned my phone calls. I felt as if I were going crazy. I drove to the Kissimmee office of HRS and demanded to talk to the caseworker who was either on vacation, out of the office, or in a meeting. She was never available to meet with me and I began to get this huge lump in my throat.

Valentine's Day arrived and Ronnie went with me to the Florida Boy's Ranch. He very sternly (if that word really describes his verbiage) stated that we were there to see our son and they had better produce him. After another very long wait for several hours, we were informed by some man who claimed he was a psychologist, that Jamie had been moved and would not be allowed to return to an abusive family and that we should just leave things alone. I thought Ronnie was going to come unglued and he just stared at him in disbelief. I asked him what on earth he was talking about. Jamie wasn't in an abusive family and all of this came about because I, not someone else, wanted to get him help. I was doing what I thought was best for Jamie by seeking counseling. No one ever came to me, claiming they were taking him because of abuse. I was told to go home, it would be checked into and they would get back with us. I was without words and Ronnie was red as an apple with anger. On our way outside Ronnie said to me, "Baby, whatever it takes, I'll get two jobs, we're gonna hire an attorney and get our son home where he belongs. As God is my witness, they won't get away with this!" I cried all the way home.

On arriving home, I called my best friend Misty and told her what had happened. Hysterical and gasping for air, I could hardly breathe, let alone talk. She told me to breathe into a paper bag. Misty was the type of person who *never* took no for an answer about anything and said she would do some checking with a couple of attorney friends of hers. She had many influential friends and maybe someone would know how to help. We talked to a couple of attorneys by phone that week who were hesitant, to say the least, regarding our entire situation. In between phone calls to attorneys, I kept calling the HRS office to find out more answers. They kept telling me they were still checking into things and to be patient. Things like this take time to sort out, especially when there has been a claim of abuse. I told them I just wanted my son back and didn't care about anything else they were trying to figure out.

The weeks strung on and I grew weary. My calls dropped from every day to every three days and then once a week to every two weeks. I was exhausted, I didn't sleep and with two other babies to tend to, I was close to giving up. Mother's day came and went and I became more and more depressed. Ronnie stayed out on the road longer and I became a robot, going through the motions of being a wife and mother. Ronnie's mother came by daily and kept telling me that things happen for a reason, and it would all work out, she was sure of it.

CHAPTER 9

DEVASTATION

O N JUNE 2, 1981, A MONTH and three days before my 26th birthday, Misty came over to see me while mom was there and said, "I'm getting you out of this house ... where do you want to go?"

I told her I needed some stuff from the store. Winn Dixie was right behind the house, so after checking with mom, we walked over. We ended up being like homeless people because we had to bring a buggy home since I bought way too much to carry. We laughed all the way to the house, praying no one we knew would see us, let alone get arrested for stealing a shopping cart. I hadn't laughed in so long and it felt wonderful.

When we walked in the door, Mom met me with a message from Diana at the Orlando HRS office. She said

I needed to call her and was informed it was important. I was so excited that I ran into the house while poor Misty brought the cart inside, God forbid anyone saw her alone with it. I called and got Diana immediately. I just knew she was going to tell me this whole mess had been a terrible mistake and I could finally come and pick up my child. That was not to be the case. She told me that she was calling to inform me that my son, Jamie, had been accidentally killed on May 18th on his bicycle when hit by a car. I couldn't breathe, I couldn't talk, my hands and head went numb, I remember Misty and Mom saying, "What, *What* is it?"

I handed the phone to Misty and I threw up. She was mumbling things I couldn't hear, I couldn't move or clean myself up, each breath was harder than the first and it was as if someone was telling me to take a breath. My mind went blank—for what period of time, I do not know. The next thing I remember was Ronnie coming home. I ran to him screaming, "Jamie's dead, Jamie's dead" and fell to the floor.

He squatted down next to me and with tears streaming down his face and said, "How, when, where, how did this happen, who told you this? It can't be true, and it's a sick joke!"

I told him I didn't know anything and described the events I could remember leading up to him coming in the door. His Mom was still there and then he called Misty to fill in the gaps (which are vague even to me now). I made dinner and tended to the girls, then went to bed. I couldn't sleep; I kept getting up, going to Jamie's room wondering how on earth something like this could happen. I wanted answers—all the details no matter how horrible. Lying on his bed, I held his pillow tightly and nothing seemed to make sense to me.

I got so angry, I paced around his room, pulling his clothes out of the dresser, smelling them, just for a hint of his scent, and then throwing them on the floor. I was spinning in circles, picking up every toy, every special item he ever owned and laid down on his bed again, falling asleep with his pillow clutched to my breast. I kept trying to piece together the time line and it hit me at 5:00 in the morning, abruptly waking me, as if I hadn't even been asleep. "This is *June*, and why after two weeks are they calling me? Where did this happen, why no call then? Where was his funeral, was *no one* there? Where was he buried?" I needed to know. The sun was coming up and I had slept for very little time, but it didn't matter.

My adrenalin had somehow kicked in high gear and then Gina woke up. I went in to change her and by then, Lisa was awake. She looked at me puzzled to make sure it was truly her mommy, not that crazy weird lady from the night before. I assured her mommy was fine and they both ran to wake up Daddy. I started breakfast and told Ronnie what my thoughts were. I told him I was calling again for answers and they better have them. He agreed, and neither of us could wait for 9:00 am. The clock struck *nine* and at 9:01, I dialed the phone. She was in a "meeting" and would have to call me back. I asked, "When will she call back, today, tomorrow, next week?" I needed answers today and I would call every 30 minutes until I got them. The woman at the other end of the phone assured me that I should have a call back before noon. We waited, watching the clock like hawks waiting for a chicken dinner.

At 10:52 am, the phone rang. It was indeed her asking as if she didn't know what I needed. I asked questions, firing them off before she could answer the first one with the phone parked between Ronnie's ears and mine. She told me to slow down as she had only one answer she could give us. She said, "I cannot tell you any of those answers you seek because of the adoption."

Ronnie and I looked at each other in bewilderment. "What adoption, my son wasn't adopted, they probably have the wrong child or family?" I began to have a tiny speck of hope. Then she proceeded to go over our names, Jamie's date of birth, etc., and we became more puzzled than before.

There had to be some sort of terrible mistake as then softy she said, "You didn't know about the adoption?"

I said, "*No*, he wasn't anywhere to be adopted, he went to the center for testing, how on earth ... what is going on?" She said she was sorry and hung up.

Now, talk about dumb founded, Ronnie and I just sat there staring at the phone. "Get her back," he said. I tried, but as we suspected, she wasn't available. What do we do now, was the only thing we could say? It was so quiet at that moment in the house. Lisa wasn't begging Daddy for a pony ride, Gina was sitting oblivious to the world playing with her "headless" Barbie doll and we just sat there. You could have heard a pin drop. It was the stillest that house had been in years and we were lost ... completely.

Ronnie called his Mom, sister and brother. I vaguely remember wandering around. Misty came over and I couldn't cry—it just wasn't real. I walked into his bedroom and Lisa followed me in. "Bubba's room is messy Mommy"—the mess I had made the night before. I said, "Let's clean it up" and she climbed on his bed, laid down and looked at me with her Daddy's big brown eyes and said, "I miss Jamie, Mommy, when is he coming home?"

How do you tell a three year old her brother is gone forever, the brother that teased her, taught her how to walk, pushed her over on purpose and loved her beyond words? I didn't know what to do, I just sat down on his bed, picked her up and told her that Bubba had gotten hurt and the Angels from Heaven came and took him to see Jesus. She said with a determined look on her face, "No Mommy, he can't live there, he 'posed to be here." With that, she got up and just walked away leaving me sitting there with tears rolling down my face.

I am not sure how I was able to function through the days that followed. I had several people around me all the time, but it didn't seem to help. Ronnie went back to work and I just existed. The people that were constantly around me had drifted away one by one and I began to sink into a deep despair. I felt as if someone had sucked the life out of me, burying me into a well of cold dark water and most of the time I didn't care if I was able to get out or not. I managed to be a mother and a wife, but just barely!

CHAPTER 10

ALTERED EXISTENCE

LISA STARTED KINDERGARTEN in the fall of 1983, two years after Jamie's death. I was heart sick and totally lost on her first day of school. Gina and I were left home alone and I had to get myself out of the house, so we went for a very long walk, to the lake and back, which was several blocks. We came home and played with her dolls. I never thought the time moved fast enough.

When Lisa arrived home from school, I felt safe, but every morning it was worse. The fear that she wouldn't come home was beginning to eat me alive and I could never find enough to do. Friday of that first week finally arrived and Ronnie came home. I had started having terrible nightmares, probably brought on by my fear of

Lisa being away at school, and I had hoped that with Ronnie tucked safely next to me in bed they would stop. It did not stop the middle of the night screams I was having and he woke me on Saturday night fighting and screaming.

"I can't reach you, I can't reach you." Ronnie asked me to remember the dream I was having.

I remember so vividly because there really wasn't much to the dream … just blackness. Jamie's hand was reaching for mine. I heard his voice, "Help me mommy, come and get me mommy, please mommy." My fingers couldn't reach his, no matter how hard I tried and stretched, I just couldn't reach him. The second dream was the same, not much content, but horrifying just the same. Jamie was in a cage, dirty, his hair was long, his clothes were tattered and torn, he wore no shoes, and he was clutching his brown raggedy stuffed monkey with stuffing falling out of a missing limb. "Help me mommy, come and get me mommy, please mommy?" I thought I was losing my mind. Ronnie would continually wake me while I was fighting and screaming, but the same dreams just repeated themselves, over and over!

Saturday morning, the next day after Lisa's first week at school, Ronnie's mom came over and said, "You two need a night out!"

I had gone over all the dreams with her and Ronnie so we all decided that the best thing to do was to get out of the house and go for a motorcycle ride. We left about seven in the evening and it was cool and refreshing. The scent of fresh crisp air and flowers assaulted my nose, the wind felt exhilarating on my face and I was at peace, if only for a few minutes. We stopped at a friend's house to see if they wanted to go for a ride where there were several people. They couldn't go for a ride, but invited us to stay and have a couple of drinks. Our friend's wife informed me that I looked like hell and I very briefly, without much detail, told her about the nightmares and not being able to sleep. I was tired, always on edge, and falling apart at the seams!

That evening, I was introduced to cocaine, that glorious drug you sniffed up your nose and it took every possible care away. That wonderful feeling of "free", no more fear … I was invincible. We stayed and I enjoyed a couple more "little" sniffs. At that time, Ronnie had no idea what I was doing, but he seemed to like me again all of a sudden. He told my friend, "Whatever you two talked about worked for her, so keep on doing it." My husband looked at me again, in love. I laughed, smiled and played. I was so happy the pain was gone. All I knew at that moment was I wanted it to last forever.

I had never experienced drugs before, always thinking how evil they were. But how could something evil make me feel so good? It made me feel as if I never had anything to worry about and I could achieve anything. It was a miracle. Ronnie enjoyed being around me, the girls seemed happier and as long as I had a "little stash", everyone and everything went great. Ronnie never asked me where the $80.00 every so often went, and I am sure he noticed that bills sometimes were late, but he didn't seem to care. We were happy in love again. I would have a little sniff in the morning and it would wear off leaving me with a hunger I cannot describe, so I would do a little more, then a little more and still, a little more. This continued for a few months until I was buying a gram a day. I just needed the "toot". I lost interest in food, friends, Ronnie, and possibly the girls, but somehow I managed to take care of them.

Misty knew what was going on and constantly nagged me to stop, until one day she told me if I didn't, she would tell Ronnie. I figured deep down he already knew, but never said anything. He was back to not caring, staying out on the road longer and longer. I tried to quit, managed to go two weeks, but then the depression kicked in. We went out on the motorcycle again for a short run and I was offered a "line". I thought to myself, "One line won't hurt anything" so up my nose it went. I went from depressed to euphoric again. I became the life of the party and followed my friend to the bathroom every time she would go. Before we left that evening, I bought some from her because the urges grew stronger and I couldn't seem to reach the high I expected. No matter how much I did, the lines were getting thicker and longer each time. I couldn't get that "first" feeling again.

I vaguely remember the next day as Ronnie finally

confronted me about it. Misty came over that Sunday, and Ronnie was getting ready to go back on the road. I heard Misty say, "So, she's given up on housework too?" I don't recall his answer, but it hit me hard in the chest and the heart. She was right.

Ronnie quickly kissed me goodbye, not on the lips but the forehead and told me to straighten up or he wasn't coming back. I got up, washed my face and through desperate tears, told Misty that I needed help. Not with the cocaine, I could quit that, but with the nightmares and the horrible pain I felt in my heart. If I could just find out where Jamie was buried, everything would start to get better.

She said she had this new attorney in Orlando and she would make a few phone calls. She would call him and see if he would talk to me, but I was to get off my butt and get my act together. I felt good about that and she helped me clean up the house, fix supper, and tuck the girls into bed. She stayed the night and we sat up most of the evening talking and trying to figure out what our plan of action would be. On Monday, she called her attorney and we made an appointment for Thursday that week. I was elated. I shook off the stupor that was nagging me from the weekend and started the day. Misty went home and I became the cleaning machine that everyone knew me to be. It was spring cleaning in action in the middle of the fall. I just knew I was going to get the answers that I needed. The next few days were OK for me. I made up my mind, "No more cocaine" and I was going to be a super mom to Lisa and Gina. I also decided that I would start going to church again, any church. I had been working for a contractor whose son was Mormon. He always looked happy and full of the spirit, so I asked him about his church. He invited us to attend on Sunday. Thinking that was a perfect idea, I decided to attend his church on Sunday with the girls. Ronnie refused to go.

Thursday arrived and Misty picked me up to drive over to Mick's office. I told him my story and, after I was done, he looked at me with the saddest look I had ever seen. He claimed I needed a family attorney to open the adoption file because he couldn't do it.

He was a personal injury attorney, but he had some friends who had access to the "back doors" of HRS and would try to find out some answers. He couldn't promise anything, and would get back to us as soon as he could. I was thrilled, thinking I was finally going to find someone to help me. He gave us the name of a family attorney and said she was very good at what she did. He didn't know her personally, but heard she was the one to get the job done. I left his office with the first ray of hope I had felt in a very long time. I was optimistic and couldn't wait until Ronnie's call later that evening. When he called, he said that he was happy to hear me sounding better. He said he checked into some property, five acres out in St. Cloud Manor. We needed to get away from that house. At this point, Jamie's room was still intact. I told him I wasn't sure about that, but we could discuss it more when he came home.

The next Friday, Ronnie came in off the road with a new piece of equipment. It was a tattoo machine and he was excited about doing tattoos saying it would give us extra money for the attorney. I thought, oh that is cool because Ronnie was very artistic and so was I. He had several drawings and this could be the beginning of watching him do his artwork firsthand.

On Sunday the girls and I trotted off to the Mormon Church for our first visit. We arrived to all these smiling faces. The children went to their church, the women went to their church, and the men went to theirs. It was OK with me, after all, I was raised Catholic and nothing could be as strict as what I was used to. Maybe less structured churches were like this.

We came home from church three hours later to find Jamie's room completely renovated into a tattoo parlor. All of Jamie's things were gone. He gave them away, everything in three hours, claiming it was time for our family to move forward. We needed the room to do tattoos, with people entering through the front door, not coming through the other side of the house. We could quickly make money for the attorney we needed to hire. I went numb. I lost my son and now all of his things were gone in a matter of a few hours. The wall that once had been blanketed with his pictures of horses, bears, and lions was now covered with black swirls of tattoo flash. The wall where his cream colored bed was, covered with Jamie's fine artwork and stickers, was replaced with a desk, chair, lamp and big black tattoo machine. His "sailboat" blue rug was replaced with an orange and black Harley Davidson rug and there was this hideous beer light blinking where his stuffed animals had been safely hung with a net. He was indeed gone. No more sign that I had a little boy with jet-black hair and big sable brown eyes. Eyes whose lashes were thick, full and long causing many a woman to envy such a beautiful attribute. Eyes that totally mesmerized those they looked into. His smile warmed any heart, especially the heart of an angry mom, like when he was found on the roof of the building with his dog.

At that moment, I turned around and saw the kitchen "adventure" passageway that only months before was covered in eggs, milk, and the entire contents of the refrigerator. It was the morning Ronnie and I awoke to a strange group of sounds, giggling, the patter of feet in motion, "wheeeee", *thump*! Ronnie had looked at me with this puzzled look and I at him, "What do you think that is?" I asked. We quietly got up, opened the door, and peeked out. In a flash, there went Lisa as she ran across the living room floor and disappeared into the kitchen, "wheeee", *thump*! Before we could ascertain, there went Gina and Jamie right behind her, assisting his baby sister as she was a bit unsteady. Giggle, Giggle, "Wheeeee", *thump*, and *thump*! We arrived into the kitchen and there stood three children who looked like they just stepped out of a horror film, as if they had been vomited from the depths of an alien. Each child was covered in two dozen eggs, oatmeal, ketchup, flour, an entire gallon of milk, pancake mix and anything else they could find in the refrigerator. As a big clump of egg-encapsulated oatmeal dripped off Jamie's ear, he proudly remarked, "We make breakfass!"

I think it began innocently enough as the big brother was going to start the morning meal. With that came clumsy fingers and eggs that fell. Then, someone slipped and did the first slide. I am not sure how the entire contents ended up on the floor but it was so funny looking at the three stooges standing there dripping with debris. We tried to appear stern, but Ronnie lost it first, erupting into a chorus of laughter, and I followed. The laughter took over the entire situation and the children came running. We flipped for the clean up. Heads got the children, tails got the kitchen, and I got tails!

Where was my little boy, the one I was remembering? Why was all of this happening to me? Why was my "little man" dead and why was looking at a place that used to resemble him all changed to a black and orange tattoo studio. I turned and went into my bedroom with such an ache of loneliness and despair. I must have cried myself to sleep because for the moment, the pain subsided.

The rest of the week went rather well, considering the weekend before. Ronnie took a couple of weeks off to get the tattoo business rolling and I went to work as usual. The weekend that followed was our opening day for tattoos. Ronnie had scheduled a motorcycle "tattoo run" beginning with some very colorful characters that used the front door directly into Jamie's room, now a tattoo parlor. While he would work, I would watch and keep the girls away, as much as I could, from the inking. Some areas of tattooing were in places I wouldn't dream of and didn't want the little ones seeing this display of individuality!

CHAPTER 11

BROKEN TRUST

R ONNIE QUIT DRIVING OVER THE ROAD and took a position with a friend of his pulling and setting up mobile homes. We decided that with Jamie's death, it would be beneficial for him to be a close at home father and husband. Between pulling mobile homes and tattooing, we were doing pretty well. While Ronnie would tattoo, I would draw things. He noticed that I had the ability for art and drawing. He decided I should try my skills at inking other people's skin, but I wasn't so sure. He had me do a panther "cover up" on his forearm first. That was easy, so he convinced me I could get a lot of practice by doing an entire back scene on him. At first, I was very hesitant, but after I began the Molly Hatchet picture from a t-shirt onto his back, it became almost fluid for me. It was easy, simple, and quite enjoyable, not to mention I really enjoyed watching him squirm sometimes! It was the scene of a woman riding a horse. We added some clouds and thus began my short-lived tattoo career. I took over the two-day weekend bike runs of tattooing while he and the girls would fix and paint Harleys. Actually, it was Lisa and Ronnie, as Gina showed very little interest in Harleys and loved Care Bears, dolls, and dresses. Lisa on the other hand had taken Jamie's "shadow" position and wanted to do everything Daddy did. She would play in his tools, get greasy helping him tear down and build motorcycles, and even showed interest in nursing by helping birth our Brindle Pit Bull, Sadie's, puppies.

The weeks flew by and we were able to make enough money to put down on five acres in St. Cloud Manor. A quiet desolate area of farmland—a place that smelled of freshness, open air, and pine trees. Ronnie was quite the thrifty shopper and came across two 12' wide mobile homes, one 30' long and the other 54' that had been damaged minimally in two separate hurricanes. He decided he could put the two damaged pieces together and make one large double wide, which he and several friends did together. Ronnie prepared the land with a borrowed backhoe, pulling palmettos, moving dirt, digging the hole for the septic tank, while his three girls watched and supervised. It was glorious, fresh air, mud for the girls to play in, and me dreaming of a home all our own and a new beginning.

Finally it was time for him to set up the mobile homes and place them side by side. The smaller one had only a slight hole in the right side from where a hot water heater had blown through and the larger one had a huge gaping hole on the left side, from what I do not know. However, he and a mass of family and friends, (Ronnie never met a stranger), accomplished the completion of our new home in one day. From the inside of the home you would never have guessed it was a mobile home, but from the outside, there was no doubt. We always had good intentions to do a roof over and siding, but that never did come to fruition.

The tattoo business stopped almost as fast as it had begun. Ronnie was working two jobs, one moving and setting mobile homes, the other at Disney's Epcot. We were making payments to an attorney at this time, and I felt things were going in the right direction.

The attorney we hired was beginning to show some promise and we were actually thinking we were on the road to a new and informative future. The light at the end of the tunnel was beginning to form and we were getting our hopes up high regarding the events and outcome of our son's death.

Our newly hired attorney filed a "Petition to reopen court file" on August 27, 1985. Depositions were scheduled to be taken and we had our first hearing before a judge in Osceola County on September 10, 1985. I remember walking into the courthouse as if it were yesterday, not 25 years ago.

The people-filled hallway outside of the courtroom was a cauldron of nervous tension; I could feel the nervous energy of everyone in the courthouse. One could smell the sweat from nerves all around as well as the sickening sweetness of cheap perfume while waiting for our turn.

The attendees to the "show" consisted of our attorney, the attorney for HRS, the judge and I. You would think they would allow my husband to be by my side, but that was not the case. I learned later on that the HRS attorney was afraid of him and Mr. X knew he couldn't badger me or intimidate me the way he'd done before if Ronnie were there.

After the formality of standing upon the judge's arrival, my attorney opened with, "Your Honor, we feel a grave injustice has occurred here. Mrs. Marshall has been stripped of her parental rights with regard to noted child; falsely accused of abuse and then the child was adopted out and has since died. She would like to find out where her child is buried, etc. for the adoption that was never to have happened, is sealed. Your Honor, we contend that this child was unwillingly removed from the home, given away for adoption illegally, and then wrongfully died in the custody of another appointed by HRS."

The judge turned to Mr. X and stated, "What is the departments answer to this?"

"Your Honor, Mrs. Marshall could not handle her child, she didn't want her child so she brought him to us."

The judge was silent for a few moments and started asking me questions regarding the age of Jamie, foster care placement papers signed, and why I sought help from them. I started to answer, but Mr. X began pounding his fist and yelling at me. "You couldn't handle your child, you didn't want him anymore, and you gave him up!"

During this mans tirade, The Judge dropped the gavel and a bit louder said to Mr. X, "Can you tell me sir, why these adoption papers weren't witnessed until two weeks after Mrs. Marshall filed the motion to review? That is four years past the date they were to be signed."

His question went unanswered as Mr. X just sneered at me and looked at the judge. My attorney told the judge, "We request the adoption file be reopened your Honor."

The Judge stated he needed to review the file and we could set another date for sometime later for hearing. He also ordered that the adoptive parents appear before him at a date I did not know, however, they never appeared and the judge stated to our attorney that they were in contempt of court.

CHAPTER 12

DESPONDENCY

DAYS, THEN WEEKS WENT BY with no phone calls and no answers. Our attorney set up depositions for all those involved and weeks became months. I continued to call her relentlessly and she did not return the phone calls. The next thing we found out was she was out due to some horrible illness. I called several times a month for two months and promptly was told she had left the firm. I was stunned, but I assumed it was related to her grave illness that they had led me to believe. I asked the young woman on the phone, who turned out to be another attorney with the firm, if someone else at their firm could take over the case, but it was not to be. No one else was aware of the case, so I asked about coming to get my file. They informed me to call back in a couple of days. I called back three days later and, as you guessed, more bad news; they could not find my file. Ms S. must have taken it with her. This file was critical to our case as it contained all important documents, including a copy of the phone bill showing when I had returned the call to HRS the day I was informed of Jamie's death, my diary with all pertinent data of names, dates, etc; as well as all birth records and miscellaneous information regarding my son.

Now you can imagine my frame of mind at this time. I could feel my pulse increasing, my temperament escalating to volcanic proportions, with thoughts of destroying the phone I held in my hand. Instead, I called Mick, Misty's attorney and left a message for him to please call me regarding this last chain of events. I was fed up with the amount of bad luck I was experiencing. It seemed every time I turned around, I ran into a brick wall with no where to go and no one to help.

The next morning after very little sleep, I tried to focus on my work. The other lady in my office had to make a trip to the bank and my boss was out of the office. I decided to call my "friend" and informed her that I was in need of more "medicine". I made plans to stop by her house quickly after work and while there, I was introduced to a brand new way of getting the "true blue" euphoric state of no more pain called "Freebasing"! I was already a cigarette smoker, so sucking on a pipe, burning cocaine was purely natural to me and yup, the pain left!!

I took to it like a baby takes to a nipple and I was off and running. I experienced relief of frustration, full of a feeling that makes you think you can take on the world. However, it was still the satanic drug it was before, only worse, because doing it was very short-lived. Similar to using it nasally, but the feeling only lasts about 30 minutes (or less) and leaves you with a much greater craving for more, much, much, more! So much more that you remain awake for two days, and every hour or so smoke up some more. It relieved the pain in the heart but left a yearning so strangely painful, you want to continue using the drug.

The next few months passed pretty much on a day-to-day basis and spiraled downhill. I did exist and go to work. Ronnie's and my marriage was steadily declining, and I was again on drugs with my husband beginning to join me. Lisa and Gina were basically taking care of themselves as Christmas arrived. I hurt so bad inside, had no God, and my marriage was collapsing. I spent the holidays as if robotic, with no feeling, using cocaine every chance I got.

In January of 1986, I was fired ... *fired!* How humiliating can life get? I stayed high for a few more days and took a job with Ronnie's boss/friend in Orlando, where he was still pulling and setting mobile homes. Jamie's name was never spoken anymore.

Now, don't get the idea that Lisa and Gina weren't happy and we didn't have good times because we did. They just weren't as prevalent in my mind as the deep dark pain that encapsulated my heart.

CHAPTER 13

CLEANSING

J ULY 2, 1986, FIVE YEARS and one month to the date
when I found out that my child was dead I wound
up, by my own admission, in a drug rehabilitation
unit. Actually, it was the greatest choice I had made for
my family and myself in all those years. I had been up
for three days straight freebasing cocaine. Each time the
girls needed me, they pounded on the door and I would
quickly get my fix and return to them. However each day
that followed, I was out less and behind a locked door,
more. On the third day Lisa managed to make sure she
and Gina had baths, and put them to bed. The fourth
morning I was done and had slept maybe three hours.
I got up and somehow managed to get the girls fed,
dressed, and ready to go the babysitters, who lived a mile

down the road from us. She was a very special person and friend who thankfully and graciously took very good care of my children. It was summer, the girls were going swimming and Vanessa said to make sure they had their bathing suits as they had just gotten a brand new above ground pool.

I drove to her house and blacked out for a moment, full of cocaine, no sleep, and no food. Startled, I realized I had almost driven the girls off a six-foot embankment into a ditch filled with water! "Oh *my God*, I almost killed us all!" A cold harsh reality swept over me like a mass of mosquitoes. I was covered in guilt, pain, and a fear so immense I could hardly breathe. I had two beautiful children still with me, alive, that needed me and I had to get my stuff together. I needed to get on with my life … real life. I knew what I had to do. I dropped the girls off and drove to Thee Door Drug Rehabilitation Center in Orlando. I stood at the front desk with tears and pleading words pouring from my heart, "I need help, please help me." I just kept crying, begging, falling to my knees as the sobs racked my entire body. A counselor by the name of Don came out and said if I were truly serious about passing through those doors to my drug free life, I would have to stay 30 days. I assured him I was there to begin living again, no matter what it took. I stepped through those doors and painfully faced my demons. They were gnawing at me like a big muddy dirty dog chewing at his fleas. I vomited, I cried, I spoke, I was counseled, I prayed until my knees bled, I screamed, and thirty days later I was cleansed body and soul.

I found God again, the real God, the one who loved me, cared for me, and died for me. I made a promise to Him and to myself that I would never go back to that kind of life again and I have kept that promise. I walked out of those doors a more alert, focused, sober person than I had been in five years. I had two beautiful daughters that needed me and although I still had a deep broken heart for my deceased son, I was going forward. I had learned so many things in there. During family time, I learned my husband had several affairs, including one with our adult babysitter, impregnating her. I took care of her throughout her pregnancy not knowing she was carrying my husband's child ... and then even after the little girl was born. She left town shortly after the birth of her child, which actually was a comical event as I look back on it now. I remember the day I found out she was pregnant. Ronnie and the girls were playing on the floor in the living room while "M" and I were talking. She had been staying with us and had serious bouts of "morning" sickness. I asked her if she might be pregnant and she told me she was.

At this point, I should have thought it strange that Ronnie turned white, choked on his tea and went to the kitchen, still within earshot mind you of the conversation. "M, I didn't realize you were seeing anyone, does the father know?"

"He didn't for a while" (I could tell she was very nervous) "because I didn't want to break up his marriage. I feel so guilty, I knew he was married, but I slept with him anyway."

Through her sobs, I held her and promised she could stay with us until she got on her feet. This was the type of person I was, a true dumb blonde. Everyone around us knew she was carrying his child. It is certainly true about the old adage that the wife is the last to know! In her seventh month, she rented a little studio apartment and moved there as I continued taking her to her prenatal appointments. I now know where the money came from for her apartment and a month after the baby was born, she moved up north to live with family.

After I left Rehab, the girls and I moved to an apartment in Orlando called Strawberry Fields. Ronnie begged me to return to him and I told him I needed time to think and begin to forgive. I had religiously returned to the Catholic Church and we attended Mass regularly. I had so many decisions I had to make. Jack, my brother-in-law was wonderful to the girls and me. One thing I can say about my husband is he was a fantastic father and never said anything negative about us to our friends or family. He always gave me more than enough money and Jack would do silly things for me so he could give me money to "tie me over". I remember one day he brought the Corvette over and asked me if I would "Karen" clean it for him while he ran errands. He returned and handed me $100.00. I told him it was too much but he said it was OK as he was sure we needed it. Jack then turned and gave the girls a big jug of nickels for them to get what they wanted.

Three months after moving to Orlando, we returned to the property as Ronnie wanted his family back where they belonged, so he moved to Winter Haven. By Christmas of 1986, we were all back together as a family in our home. We hired another attorney for the adoption case and I started college to keep my mind busy. First I had no particular goal in mind, but decided to go into psychology to see if maybe I could learn about children and see if I would be able to help children as confused as my son was. Lisa and Gina enjoyed our clean happy family and even thought it was cool that mommy had to sit and do homework like they did. Ronnie stayed busy and went to work for a construction company in St. Cloud. He was tickled to be driving heavy equipment and he loved working outdoors.

We were united as a family, attending church every weekend, and maintaining contact with our attorney who would continually say, "nothing new." I prayed for patience from God. I wasn't as consumed with it any longer since I had learned to give it over to Him. I knew it would also be a matter of time and I would at least know where my little man was buried so I could put some closure to that chapter for a while, knowing that at least someday, I would see him again.

Before I knew it, three years passed. We seemed to have a happy family until November 1989 when my husband didn't come home. I lay awake all night worrying where he might be, was he hurt, had something happened? Finally two days later he strolled in to tell me he wasn't as strong as me and was using cocaine again. I begged him to get help and he stated that we can't afford it now, but if I just try and be patient, he can kick the habit. I know the wave of depression this causes and I told him that I could not be around it. He promised me he would stop, and he did, staying away from his friends that used drugs and all went well for another nine months.

The day before Gina's 11th birthday, a nightmare, while awake, ruptured our peaceful family. I went to get my hair permed and Janice, Ronnie's sister, was watching the girls. The beautician is a friend of hers and she doesn't take that long. When my hair was done, I didn't want her to style or dry it because it was already 7:00 pm and I wanted to get home to start supper. I paid and thanked her, and went to get the girls. I sat and chatted with Janice for about thirty minutes and left.

We laughed and played on the way home. The girls were teasing me about my stinky hair. When we walked into the house, it was dark and eerily quiet with absolutely no noise. I knew Ronnie was home since his motorcycle was in the driveway, not put away in the shed as he always did. I assumed he had come home from work and laid down to rest from working in the hot sun all day. Lisa and Gina decided that meatloaf sandwiches would be a great idea for dinner. I got the girls situated in the kitchen eating and went to ask Ronnie if he was hungry. I tapped him on the shoulder and softly said, "Ronnie, do you want to get up and have a sandwich?"

He rolled over and an explosion occurred. It was as if he were possessed by Satan. He jumped out of the bed, grabbed me by the throat and threw me up against the wall. At that moment, I could only think of survival and I started scratching and kicking while he was screaming "Who have you been with, you been out f-ing someone," … on and on and on.

Lisa came running in screaming, "Daddy *no!*" I managed to get away and he chased me down the hall grabbing my hair. I fell as he began kicking me and at this point, Lisa climbed on him to try and get him to stop. He pushed her and I got crazy with him yelling, "Ronnie, snap out of this, this isn't you, stop, *stop!*"

He got this very bizarre look on his face and walked into the bedroom. I heard the cabinet open and I knew he was getting the gun. He previously ripped the phone out of my hand and I told Lisa and Gina to go to the neighbor's house and call the police. They did not leave until Gina saw her father with the gun. She ran out of the house and Lisa stood there, with her eyes wide open and crying, watching her father point the gun at me.

"No Daddy", almost a whisper, then screams, "*No Daddy!*"

I realized that he was not himself; he was riddled with drugs and not aware that the people he loved more than anything in the world were about to be harmed by him. I couldn't think and all I said was, "Ronnie, you don't want to do this, your baby is watching you." He froze up and I don't know if it was the siren or Lisa, but he walked into the kitchen and sat down. I grabbed Lisa and Gina, who were outside on the porch sobbing hysterically, and we got in the car.

As I was trying to pull out, the police stopped me. I told them, "I'm not staying, I don't care what they're saying, I am leaving and they can follow." The girls were both crying and I drove off with an officer following me. I pulled over about two miles away and I gave him the events as quickly as I could. I told him we we're going to Janice's house and I gave him the phone number. Back in those days, the man is not arrested, no one is. The police talked to him, and the next day, with the help of police officers, I gathered up our things and moved to my brother's house in Auburndale.

Ronnie was sober and straight the Saturday that followed and, with great remorse, helped me move the furniture over to Auburndale. He promised me he would get help and I told him I prayed he would. Life is too short to go around hurting people and himself. He agreed.

CHAPTER 14

MOVING FORWARD

A NEW ADVENTURE BEGAN FOR the girls and I—no drugs, no anger, no terror, just a new beginning. Ronnie did manage to get clean and in the process ended up in Federal prison for ten years. That is a story in itself; one that taught my daughters that crime doesn't pay!

I took a job as a hostess at a local restaurant in Winter Haven and went to college. I already had a surgical tech degree, but I wanted to be a nurse and needed the school and time to continue. The girls and I moved to Thornhill Road in Winter Haven after my brother had to sell his house in Auburndale. I went to work for a local hospital in 1992 as a scrub tech and continued Nursing School.

Lisa, Gina, and I managed to make Tuesday our "sit

down dinner night" because of our busy schedules. They thought it was pretty cool that all of us had homework to do every night, since most of the time we didn't spend a whole lot of time together. We were in the same house, just doing different things. Lisa became my study buddy and managed to learn a lot about human anatomy. Gina was involved with her favorite pastime, television. She managed to do her homework, but it truly wasn't her favorite way to spend her time. I would have to nag her and she would just say, "Oh, mom. Just because you decided to go back to school doesn't mean I have to work that hard at it." Both Lisa and Gina were involved with cheerleading and Lisa took on Band in two separate forms, marching band which required her to stay after school on Wednesdays and the games every Friday, and symphonic band, managing to remain in first chair until her senior year when she actually had to fight for it. She and Gina were involved with clogging and many other outside activities which required me to be a very busy, traveling mom. The car was wearing down and I couldn't wait for Lisa to be old enough to get her license.

November 14, 1992 hit me like a ton of bricks. It was Jamie's 18th birthday and I felt like the black hole was chasing me again. Lisa and Gina realized that Mom's heart was in danger and reminded me that I had the greatest support team, not only my children but my wonderful nursing instructors as well. No one in the school knew the circumstances; they just knew I had a little boy that died.

Christmas that year was very difficult as well. Money was very low. Ronnie was in prison, and there was no child support. I had to make a choice between bills and food over presents but thankfully my two children were more adults than most adults I knew. I had been working on Christmas Eve and came home to see two beautiful daughters greeting me with Cheshire cat smiles on their faces and their hands behind their backs. They got out the Christmas decorations, lights and all and decorated a very large plant like a Christmas tree. No tears, no crying for gifts that weren't there, just smiles and hand made presents for their mom made out of a cut up sheet. I was never more proud of anyone in my life! I also was re-convinced of God's power when Christmas morning arrived and there was a miracle on our doorstep ... presents for my children and myself. I know as I live and breathe, that it was my nursing instructor, Linda, who was responsible. God's miracles often come through His genuine special people.

I actually began living again with the help of friends, family, my counselor, Father Caulfield, and God. They all helped me to accept that when God was ready for me to know the how and why of what took place, He would let me know.

In August of 1996, my best friend, my brother, died in an accident and I met my wonderful best friend, Denys. She was another gift from God, appearing in my life when I really needed someone like her. She understood things that even some of my dearest and closest family members didn't, because she and I were at the same point in our lives. We shared common goals. She was a paramedic getting ready to attend LPN school and I was just a RN, fresh out of school that May. Denys allowed me to be myself. She helped me to open up, and helped take the bitterness away because she allowed me to talk openly. I felt like I could, for brief moments, not feel guilty for getting help for my son. She allowed me to sit in silence with my own thoughts, which to me was an expression of understanding for having shared with her a valuable portion of my life and of myself. Denys never judged me, my actions or decisions and I in turn allowed her to grow and develop on her own terms, minus my constant pushes in her schooling that got her through LPN school and then RN school.

In November of 1996 at our family Thanksgiving dinner, Lisa and her husband, Kevin announced to me that I was going to be a grandma sometime in July. I was so excited and thrilled to know new life was joining the family. Lisa and Gina, sisters who through the teenage years decided to hate each other, became friends again. I smiled as they giggled and spoke tenderly to each other discussing the baby to be born. "My first grandchild," I thought to myself, "If Jamie were alive, I could have already been a grandma."

A small tear fell down my cheek and Lisa looked at me with her uncanny ability to read my mind and said,

"You're thinking about Jamie, aren't you?"

I just nodded as she walked over to me and gave me a loving hug saying, "I am sure Jamie is happy for us."

"I believe he is and I am sure he will watch your little one grow!"

I loved being a nurse and taking care of others. It did me a world of good to help those who needed me. My children were getting on with their own lives and it helped to fill the void of them not being around.

CHAPTER 15

ATTORNEY MAYHEM

NEW YEARS DAY 1993 ARRIVED and as most people know, there are no Holidays in the operating room. We had one procedure to do on a local Polk County attorney, Mr. M, and while I was pre-oping him for the O.R. and starting his I.V., he stated to the group of us, "If you ever need legal advice I am just a phone call away. I appreciate all that you are doing."

I thought about his statement for a brief moment and jokingly told him, "Lawyers and medical personnel are not truly synonymous with each other, you know!" We all had a good laugh about that and if he would already have been pre-medicated, I would not have given his statement another thought. However, I couldn't pass up the idea that maybe someday in the future, if he were really serious, I may take him up on his offer and see what he could find out for me. However, the moment at hand really only concerned him and his upcoming surgery.

Five months later I heard Mr. M was back to work at his office and I called him. I had thought seriously about his offer for the entire five months and decided to make an appointment. Three days later I walked into his very small, stuffy dark office. I was leery at first to say the least. There was no one at the reception desk at 9:00 in the morning and I felt as if there was no one else around. He must have heard me come in the door and hollered out loud in a deep boisterous voice for me to come around to his office. I walked to my left to see this same attorney I had met at the hospital sitting with piles of folders and papers on the huge dark mahogany desk. The papers and files were so numerous one could hardly even see the top of the desk.

He was a very large man who didn't seem to fit there no matter how large the desk or office was. There was a very small window behind him, casting an eerie morning gray light. It was something you would probably have pictured seeing in a 1930's movie. I almost turned to leave but thought to myself, "If I walk away and he is the one it takes to get the adoption file opened or overturned, I will never forgive myself. I at least need to talk to him."

I looked at him as he peered above the glasses that seemed too small for his face and I asked him, "Were you serious the day of your surgery when you said you would help us if we needed it, or was it just something to say to fill the void of time?"

He replied, "Yes, I was serious, but it also depends on what it is you need. Why don't you sit down and tell me what is going on, and I will see if I can help you."

I related to him the short version of my story, just the part that my child was stolen, adopted, and died. This was all in a matter of six months and here it was 13 years later. I had hired many attorneys to no avail and all I wanted was to know where my son was buried. After a few moments of silence, he told me to bring what paperwork I had and he would review everything. He would do some research on statutes and get back with me. He told me I could call him in about ten days. Unfortunately, my file along with all my information was beginning to dwindle from all the consecutive attorneys who lost or misplaced papers vital to my case. I put what I had into two separate envelopes, one 8 ½ x 11 inch white floppy sealed envelope that went inside a mailing envelope 11 x 14 size. The outer envelope was sealed with mailing tape with my name, address, and phone number on the outside for easy access. When I walked into his office with this very precious package, his secretary raised up her arm to retrieve it from me. I was hesitant to hand it to her, yet I said, "Please take very good care of this. It is priceless to me, it's probably most of what I have left and cannot afford to lose anymore of it."

She assured me she would as she was walking it into the attorney's office at that very moment. You would think that with all the experience I had with so many attorneys, I would have made multiple copies of all of this stuff and they would be lying around everywhere, except this was not the case. Oh, there were some copies that I kept and never let out of my sight, but the ones I handed to her were equally as important. I had only one copy left of most of the file and it was now placed in her hands for safe keeping.

Exactly ten days later, I called him to see if there was any exciting news. The reply I received was, "No word yet." I was not all that disappointed mind you as I had heard those words many times before. I continued working and just let him do his job. I called approximately every one to two days for about two and a half weeks and then once every three weeks to a month. The anticipation of again finding no answers was distressing me, but I kept busy with school, work, and the girls. I assumed he would call me if he stumbled on some breath-taking, earth-shattering news.

I graduated RN school in May of 1995 and my phone calls to him had dwindled to probably every two months. I called again a few more times and then around November of that same year during my call, his secretary put me on hold. I was between cases in the operating room having lunch so I thought, "Wow, maybe he has something to tell me."

With a tiny bit of excitement, I waited. About five minutes later she came back on the phone and said, "Who are you again and what is this about?"

I was so angry, I almost couldn't stand it, but I said, "Never mind," and hung up. I had patients to take care of and went back to work. I was beginning to feel I was never going to find my baby boy's grave or the answers I sought for so long.

That evening I was telling my daughter Lisa the horribly disgusting events of the day and she said, "Hey Mom, we have this new child coming whose dad is an attorney. What do you think if I ask him about it or see if he will look at the stuff?"

I said, "I don't care, it couldn't hurt, it seems I am batting zero with my choices." I was also becoming numb and my attorney confrontations were practically ritualistic. They claim they will look at my information, see if there is anything they can do, and get back with me. The end result was always the same, "No news yet."

I met Father John Caulfield in December of 1994 and he became my direct line to God. I was beginning to live again and I started to pray like I had never prayed before, with my whole heart and soul. Father Caulfield and I had many, many talks and I began to feel tiny rays of hope in my heart. I told him everything from start to finish with Jamie's case and he was aghast that someone could experience such an ordeal.

One month, almost to the day of Lisa's conversation

with me, I walked into yet another attorney's office. The atmosphere here was much different than the previous attorney's office and there were actually two receptionists with awesome inviting smiles. I said I was there to visit with Mr. C, and the next thing I knew we were discussing my situation at great length. He told me that due to the nature of the situation, and it being family law, I would do better with his partner. His partner had dealings with the Department of Family and Child Services before and if anyone would know where to go or whom to talk to, it would be him. He asked me three times with a raised eyebrow and concern in his voice, "They actually called you and told you your child was dead?"

I had all the evidence and paper work and I assured him they indeed did that. "I want only to know where he is buried. I don't care who adopted him right now or anything else, I just need to see for myself and sit down where his body is laid to rest." I made an appointment for a week later, and met with Attorney Mike Farrell, my attorney of record now.

Mike and I talked at great length and he told me about a case where he had already faced off with DCF and won. He told me to go and get my file, yet again, and we set another appointment for the following day. I gave him a small retainer of $500.00 and off I went to get the file, feeling a little too optimistic. I called Mr. M's office and spoke with the secretary. "Please have my file ready as I am coming tomorrow to pick it up."

She responded by saying, "Why are you picking it up?"

I said, "Because it is my file, he hasn't done anything for me in two years and I am coming to get it."

The following day, I arrived at Mr. M's office and I asked her for the file. She said, "There isn't any file, just this envelope."

I gasped and almost fell over. I felt the heat generating in my body to extreme proportions, creeping up my body, into my neck and up to my face. I think my hair even began to tingle as I realized that it was the same mailing envelope that I had taken to him two years previous and it had never been opened. This attorney endorsed all I had ever heard that was negative about attorneys. I thanked her, left his office and felt as if I needed to wipe the refuse off of my feet before getting into my car.

I walked into Mike's office and he saw the look on my face, "What happened, why do you look like you are ready to fire someone, should I be worried?"

He was half joking with me, yet he knew something serious was going on. Holding the sealed envelope in my hand, I explained to him what had happened. "He's had this for two years?"

Mike said, "What did he say to you regarding it?"

I told Mike, "I didn't speak to him and it is just as well. I was so mad that I probably would have slapped him. I just took the envelope from his secretary and left. I think back now to those four little chats I had with his office and only one with him. It explains the responses to my case he made each time of, 'Nothing new.' No kidding, he actually did *nothing!* He never even opened the outer envelope or read any of the documents. What a jerk."

At this point, I was frustrated, disillusioned, afraid, and at the end of my rope. I trusted no one and believed in no one and here I was again about to embark on yet another trek with another attorney. I left his office and went straight to Father Caulfield's at St. Joseph's Church. I updated him at great length about all that was going on and he told me to pray about it. Father sent me to the Adoration Chapel for an hour and when I returned, I felt refreshed for I had left a bucket or more of my tears at the alter. Father said to me, "God gives us many choices, sometimes we don't pick the right ones, but this attorney's name is Farrell, you say?"

"Yes, Father."

"Well, with a good Irish name like Farrell, we can't go wrong, now can we?"

I laughed looking into Father's smiling eyes that twinkled and things didn't seem so bad anymore.

CHAPTER 16

DATA YIELDS

EVENTS BEGAN TO HAPPEN, little by little. Mike went to the Osceola County Courthouse and discovered many discrepancies in the court documents. He filed a motion for discovery, which of course, was denied. He filed again, but too much time had passed. He dug some more and found my first attorney, Miss S who disappeared with an abrupt illness. He wrote her a letter and of course, she couldn't remember me, or the case, or anything pertaining to it. Things were rolling and I was getting excited, again. I felt as though I might find the light at the end of the tunnel. I was going to be able to know, and sit at my baby boy's grave telling him I was sorry I let him down. I allowed those horrible people to tell me they were going to help us and instead, I would be sitting at my precious baby's grave. It all seemed so surreal.

I began to dream of that moment and tried to think about what I was going to really say. I knew deep down he already knew my pain, but the guilt of letting those monsters into our life was overwhelming. I let go of my baby for a moment and here I was 22 years later still full of unrequited guilt. Father Caulfield told me I needed to forgive myself, but I didn't know how that could happen. I knew the beginning would be me sitting where his little body was buried for a start.

Mike was awesome and relentless. He got documents that led to documents and then hit a brick wall after filing a motion to have the adoption file opened. The judge said he needed more evidence explaining why it should be opened and we kept coming up empty handed. I could not believe how many times we would get close, only to have the door closed yet again, in our faces. I have to tell you that Mike is one of the few I started to believe in. I knew if there was going to be a way, he was not going to be the one to let me down.

I remarried again in August of 2001 to a man that Ronnie and our family had known for 22 years. Unfortunately, the marriage had no future and it lasted a very short time. I don't know if it was the loneliness in life I was experiencing or the emptiness without Ronnie, but I went against everyone's advice, especially my best friend, Denys who told me it was a mistake to marry him. I married him anyway. Denys never lets me forget that she told me so and even now, when we talk about that mistake, she gloats.

CHAPTER 17

TRIBULATION

IN MARCH OF 2002, MY MOTHER, Eunice, became deathly ill and for two months I focused only on taking care of her with my two sisters, Denise and Susan. Every other day I traveled the 100 miles to the nursing home in Altamonte Springs where my mother was admitted after her release from the hospital. She was initially placed there for rehabilitation, but in the beginning of May it was apparent that she was not going to get any better and they moved her to the Hospice side of the facility.

I have to say that the facility and people associated with Hospice are definitely members of God's angel squad! Mom received such gentle, tender-loving care in our absence and to be honest, even when we were there.

My mother had suffered with lung disease for many years related to smoking 50 plus years, and those cigarettes had finally come to take her life. Jamie had been the apple of her eye, possibly because he was her first grandchild or maybe just because we lived with her for a while after he was born. Whatever the case may have been, I knew they would soon be together again, laughing, playing, and reading stories.

Mom had this uncanny ability to be very weird at times. To handle grief, she did the strangest thing the year Jamie died. She arrived on my doorstep on November 14, 1981, Jamie's birthday, with a cake in tow that she had baked for him with seven candles included, and set it on the table. She lit the candles and sang "Happy birthday to you…"

I told her, "Mom, don't you think that is a little morbid?" I was on a terrible roller coaster and the black hole that kept threatening me was again welling up in my throat to the point of vomiting.

However, my mother just started laughing, not a sinister type of laugh, but the laugh that comes from deep down within and said, "I think he loves it. We never did the normal thing where Jamie was concerned and I think it is totally appropriate because he knows we love and miss him!"

She just kept laughing with a mischievous twinkle in her eye and I have to admit, I laughed out loud at the silliness, which indeed made me feel better too. Lisa and

Gina totally enjoyed it as well, especially eating birthday cake before dinner and I truly believe that is the reason that he grew up with them in their minds. My mother certainly knew what she was doing for a grieving family. Now I have to say, this may not be appropriate for any other person experiencing the same event, but it certainly worked for us!

On May 10th, I went to visit her at the Hospice center and she seemed partly connected to reality and partly somewhere else. I was helping her eat her cheerios (one of her favorite cereals of all time) and she looked at me with dark emerald eyes and calmly stated, "Jamie's not dead."

"What?" I was puzzled to say the least and wanted her to explain that statement.

She just continued to eat slowly and then began to cry. I asked her, "What is wrong, Mom, what do you need, are you in pain, what can I do, what is it you want?"

She looked at me so sadly with tears streaming down her face and her hands clenched together in her lap, "I don't know what I want, Karen?"

Those were the last words my mother would speak to me. I washed her face, helped her into bed, kissed her cheek, and went home with sadness so deep I cannot describe it. She slipped into a coma and never spoke to anyone else. When I left the center that day, I threw my cigarettes in the garbage outside the door and never touched them again. I knew I didn't want to suffer like her, I didn't want to fight for every breath and knew that I had just been watching my future if I didn't quit now.

I was at work, an hour away, when Denise called me and said, "Karen, she's fading fast, you need to get here if you want to see her alive one last time."

She couldn't phone me from Mom's room, as the phone was full of static, breaking up badly. She said she had to go out to the parking lot and call me. Her phone disconnected again. I was in the locker room of the hospital preparing to leave when she called me back a few minutes later. It was as in a whisper, "She's gone, Karen. While I was out in the parking lot calling you, she went."

I couldn't speak. I was not ready to let her go. I needed more time. I needed more answers. I couldn't understand things without my mother. I needed her to help me cope. I needed her laugh (no one could laugh like she did, that complete deep down belly laughter). I felt lost, kicked in the gut and had nowhere to go. What was I going to do, who was I going to talk to about Jamie and who was going to keep me grounded when the crap just kept coming with no answers?

A friend took me home and stayed with me for a while. I managed to get through the funeral with Lisa and Gina by my side, almost as if in a dream-like state. I remember little emotion, yet remember every word, ever step, and every condolence. I was sad, yet I had this bizarre sense of peace because as I laid my head down that evening, I pictured Jamie William curled up in my mother's loving arms. Neither of them was alone and my baby was safe in the arms of someone he knew and loved from down here on Earth.

CHAPTER 18

ENLIGHTENMENT

"**OH, MY GOD, I FOUND HIM.**" Jamie in black and white, blue, yellow, and green all over the page—looking for Lisa, Gina and his birth mother ... "*Me*"!

Wow, I couldn't breathe, I stood up, I sat down, and I stared. I stood up, I sat down again ... three times, and then I ran into the bedroom where my husband was sleeping.

"I found him, I found him, get up!" I screamed, "You have to get up, I found him!"

He groggily replied, "That's good honey, I knew he would be back. What? Oh no, not the duck? *Jamie?*" We had three baby ducks and one of them had wandered away. He thought that was what I was talking about.

"Jamie, I found Jamie!"

He sat up startled, then jumped out of bed and came into the office. He started to take the mouse and I screamed, "*No*, don't touch it."

He said to me sort of giggling, "Hit print, print it."

"Oh, yeah, good idea!"

There, coming out of the printer on paper in front of my very own eyes, in color, was my son. Posted years ago, when I am not sure, but posted just the same.

"I found him. Oh my God ... he's *Alive!*" I was stunned. I couldn't move or speak for a moment. I screamed, I laughed, I cried, and I threw up, again. This time because he was alive, not dead. Those bastards! 23 years I believed him to be dead. A million emotions ran through my entire body in a matter of seconds. "Thank you *mom!*"

I called Lisa. It was now one thirty in the morning, and she answered. I spoke so fast that she couldn't catch up. "What, who, when, where?" All questions I didn't take the time to answer and I hung up.

I called Gina, but she didn't answer. She never answered anyone calling in the middle of the night. I called Ronnie, "What, who, where?"

The million-dollar question became, "where?" Lisa was frantically trying to call me back and finally reached me on the cell phone since I was still on the phone with her Dad. I explained that we did a people search on the internet and found a person with the same name living in Jacksonville, Florida. Great, he was at least in Florida and everyone agreed that we would all talk after I called Jacksonville at six in the morning. I couldn't call this early with this kind of news, could I?

My husband went back to bed. Lisa, Ronnie, and I all hung up the phones and I sat there in dead silence at three o'clock in the morning staring at a piece of paper that held a few of the answers. Questions in the hundreds kept running at high speed in my mind. This piece of paper I held in my hands had only 59 answered questions of 152 pieces of information. Most of the answers were zero, none, or unknown." I willed it to speak to me, yet I couldn't seem to find or hear any reply.

I was exhausted, yet anxious. "What do I say? Jamie, this is your mother. No, wait, your biological mother ... hmmmm ... someone who loves you very much and has never stopped loving you. What happened, how were you adopted, by whom, when, where, did you have an accident on your bicycle when you were six, are you maimed, disabled...?"

"Oh, my God, did they hurt you, are you safe?"

My mind couldn't catch up with my thoughts and "it" couldn't catch its breath. I was still awake at five thirty in the morning trying to will myself to take a nap, yet I couldn't. I was afraid if I fell asleep, I would not wake up to call at six and I couldn't call this early, I wouldn't do that to him. So, I just sat there in the dead silence, listening to the fast pace of my own blood cursing through my veins.

Shortly after 5:07 in the morning (my last time looking at the clock), I must have dozed off with my face planted frontally on my desk. My husband tapped me at 5:52 am and asked me if I had been up all night. I told him I don't recall what I had done or whether I had slept or not. I was "drunkenly awake" in a stupor, yet I listened as the clock ticked very loudly those last eight minutes before the phone call.

Exactly 6:01 am I dialed the number I had acquired in Jacksonville. "Doo, doo, doo, we're sorry the number you have dialed is not in service at this time. Please consult your directory or dial "0" for operator assistance."

I stared at the phone; "You have got to be kidding me, to get this close and now this. What is this, some sort of cruel joke? Now what do I do?" I said out loud.

Square one, I called Lisa and told her the bad news. She told me to send her the pages by email and she would look them over to see if she could find anything further. I agreed and called their Dad to let him know the bad news. He told me to keep him posted, that we would find him now that we know he is alive. I was disappointed that no connection was made and stopped breathing for a moment as the reality began to really hit me. My son wasn't dead.

All those lies, all those hurtful, horrific monstrous lies. I got screaming mad and for an instant I wished I had an army tank in my possession to squash the people responsible for doing this to me. I was crying hysterically, yet laughing. Nothing made any sense. I couldn't get my thoughts together. It was as if someone had taken a million piece puzzle, thrown it up into the air and told me I had only five minutes to assemble it in order. I washed my face as if in a trance, got in the car and drove to St. Joseph's Catholic Church. I had to talk to Father Caulfield, I knew talking to him and spending time on my knees with God would help me to re-collect my thoughts. I needed a new direction for my thinking process, because where I was headed wasn't healthy for me or for those responsible!

After an hour and a half of sitting there in the chapel, it hit me again. My baby boy was alive and the tears began to flow. I was afraid the tears were never going to stop.

They were tears of anger, tears of joy, tears of frustration, tears of pain, tears of deep down joy, tears of horror, tears of hate, but wait, I realized … I didn't need to find a grave. I didn't need to have the court open the adoption. All I needed was to find him and I would get all the answers I was seeking. "Thank you God! Thank you Mom!"

I got up off my knees, marched out of that church with my head held high, right over to Mike's office. I told him what I had found and again we were full force with a vengeance. Mikes eyes shone like lit up embers of coal. "Let's get on this, if you talk to him, let me know."

"Oh, I will.

You can bet your life I will call you right away."

I arrived back home around eleven in the morning. I had to catch a few winks since I was utterly and completely drained. I was worried because I didn't actually recall the drive home. I felt almost robotic, void of any emotion and spent. My sense of security and direction was empty. I couldn't move, yet I couldn't stop thinking. I remember sitting down on the side of the bed pleading with God, "Please turn off my brain, if only for a few moments. I am unable to function in this state."

I managed to pick up the phone and call in sick to work. I had no way to explain anything nor did I have the strength to do so. Where would I begin? I had long ago started telling people I had only two children because the pain of going through the story was too much to bear and I wasn't ready to do it now. Oh, I did for a while, but each time the pain of the story began to weigh me down with the sense I might lose my sanity with the return to drugs becoming a real possibility. I chose to save myself and tell the story I had been telling for years. Only a select few of my closest friends and family knew the truth. Now, I couldn't take care of myself at the moment, let alone patients in the operating room. It would all have to wait, just for a little while longer.

CHAPTER 19

CONNECTION

I MUST HAVE DRIFTED OFF TO SLEEP because the next thing I remember was picking up a ringing phone. Lisa was crying on the other end. "Mom, I just talked to his adoptive mother and she wants to talk to you?"

"What?" I shook some of the stupor off, trying desperately to absorb what she was saying to me. "Where, what do you mean, you just spoke to his adoptive mother?" Those words, adoptive mother, cut deep into my being. I was spouting questions off at her so fast she couldn't keep up. "Where is he?"

"He's in jail."

"What jail, why?"

"I don't really know all of it, but Sharon wants to talk to you. She said Jamie's been looking for us for a really long time and he will be so excited that we found them?"

"How *did* you find them?"

"Well, the email that you sent me that Jamie filled out said he was a manager of a record store. I searched it and found it to be in Melbourne, so when I checked for the phone number, I found it. I called the record store and just asked for him. She said that he wasn't there and could she take a message. Mom, I almost fainted as I told her that I was his biological sister and was looking for him. I asked her if there was a number where I could reach him. She was quiet for a moment, almost breathing and not speaking, but then she told me she was his adoptive mother and knew this day would come. We talked for a long time. I told her how we found them and she said that he calls her from jail every Sunday night and he would be so excited to know that she spoke with us."

I was stunned, again. "Adoptive Mother ... how am I to feel about that? What do I feel about that? What do I say? Can I be objective?" I didn't want to hurt anyone, especially innocent people, so I had to think clearly to ask God for guidance, as I dialed her number. The awkwardness was overwhelming.

"Hello", she answered.

"Hello, is this Sharon?"

"Yes, is this Karen?"

"Yes, it is, Lisa gave me your number and said you wanted to speak to me about Jamie?"

"Yes, please hold on, I am at the store and I need to go to a private phone in the back, is that ok?"

"Certainly, thank you for talking to me."

God must have been reminding me to breathe because I am sure I was struggling with it. I just listened to her tell me when she adopted him, about the first day she saw him. He seemed lost and starving for affection, with those big bright brown eyes and thick long lashes. She had always wanted children but couldn't have any. If she told me what the reason was, I do not recall. Her husband, Frank, had two grown daughters from a previous marriage and she knew that Jamie was meant to be her son.

The adoption was final on April 9, 1981. The date and speed of it didn't seem to register at that moment in my mind, but it was only five months from the date he had been taken to the Boys' Ranch and only one month before they told me he died. She told me about a little cowboy outfit she purchased for him when they brought him home and about his being in jail. He had apparently been troubled since the adoption, maybe from the circumstances of his being placed for adoption, and was in and out of trouble throughout his teenage years. We made an appointment to meet in a restaurant in St. Cloud the following weekend, which would be halfway from our house to theirs, so we could talk. She would bring me pictures of him growing up.

Nothing ever prepared me in life for that day, that

conversation, or the incredible waves of emotions I encountered in just a few moments. I am certain God had his Angels working overtime with me because I am not sure a human heart can endure such an occurrence alone.

I truly cannot recall what happened next. I do know the remaining energy of my body was obliterated. I called Lisa and spoke with her briefly, touching the highlights and asked her to call her Dad and Gina. She said she would as I was frozen in place and time. The million pieces of the puzzle were spiraling around in my brain at a rate I am sure is beyond anything human. I had only one word left in my vocabulary, "Why?"

One week later, I met Sharon and Frank at the restaurant in St. Cloud. In my hand, I held pictures of my "little man" growing up from school on to his getting married. I wasn't sure what I was supposed to feel, but here was this stranger who had raised my baby boy all these years, yet instantly I felt warmth and a wonderful connection that I am sure only a mother understands. She genuinely loved "our" son and I could not hold her responsible. I mean after all, she didn't know about the horror I had experienced, did she? I felt not.

I told them I would not rest until I found out the truth and that those responsible would pay dearly. I had not given up my child for adoption no matter what they believed or how they acquired him. Yet, I sincerely thanked them for loving and protecting him. Frank looked at me and said words I will never forget, "You found him now and you have him back, let it go. You don't want to open up Pandora's Box, more people could get hurt which will cause more hurt."

I assured him I wasn't afraid of Pandora's Box and I had nothing to hide! They had already hurt me; I certainly couldn't see how much more hurt could be placed on my family or me. I would find the answers to those many questions. Someone was going to explain why my son was taken, why they broke my heart and the hearts of my family.

We parted friends, even joking with Frank on how I owed him a new drill because Sharon got a little boy when he wanted a new drill. Since I had my son back, he felt I owed him the drill. We laughed and I truly intended to purchase a drill for him, but unfortunately, the events began to spiral and I became totally engrossed with the work at hand. He never did get a drill that I am aware of, just struggles with poor health and a disrupted family.

CHAPTER **20**

ASSOCIATES

I RETURNED TO WORK ON MONDAY, June 16, 2003, full of nervous energy and a couple of hours earlier than my scheduled time. I had no idea how I was going to start explaining why I told people all those years that I had only two children and now I have a third, one that was dead but now alive. It sounded so surreal even to me, and I wasn't sure where to start. I made my way to my boss' office since I figured I should tell her first and fill her in on all of this.

I sort of peeked at her around the corner, "Do you have a moment, or should I say a lot of them?"

She raised her eyebrows curiously, motioned for me to come all the way into her office and stated she had time, "I am all ears." I knew she was not ready for the story she was about to hear.

I started slowly and then as if my mouth went into hyper speed, I blurted 23 years of information at her within 15 minutes. Ms. M's mouth was agape and her eyes were about to explode out of her head with wide-eyed blueness. "What did you just say and this time say things a bit slower please."

I slowed it down and hit the high points again, as if there were any points that were not extreme. Unfortunately for her, the leaking from my eyes had become lake filling and I was for the first time telling someone my deepest pain. I told her I intended to find the entire truth about what happened to my son, especially the person who sadistically made the decision to inform me that my little boy had died. Ms. M was so tender and supportive. She told me she would help with whatever she could, and as long as it did not interfere with patients or my work, all would be fine. I wasn't ready to announce it to the entire staff yet when she said, "You don't have to; all you have to do is process this and find someone to talk to."

I did find someone to talk to, she was the Employee Assistance Counselor provided by the hospital. Later into the chaos, I found a wonderful counselor who specialized in posttraumatic stress. She helped me start to put the puzzle together, if only in my mind, with the very few pieces of information I had. We eventually, as the information started to come in rapidly, picked up the pace to my heart reconstruction and I thank God for giving me the gift of Trudy R.

I was working two jobs at that time, which helped me keep my mind from spiraling too far out of control. From six in the morning until one in the afternoon I worked at one hospital across town in the recovery room, and from three to eleven in an operating room at my "home" hospital. I had little time to think about my troubles or myself and the time passed quickly.

I remember so clearly the day that I announced the rebirth of my baby boy. It was Friday, June 27, 2003, at exactly 1635. I was exceptionally happy during a surgical case and one of the surgeons said to me, "Karen, you sure appear to be on cloud nine. I don't think I have ever seen you this bubbly or glowing. Did you win the lottery or something?"

"No, sir, I did not win the lottery … it's something much better than winning the lottery."

"What could be better than winning the lottery," he asked.

"Finding my son alive after 23 years of believing him to be dead. He was abducted at the age of six."

The operating room went completely silent for a moment. "I guess that indeed is better than winning the lottery or anything else I can think of. Wow, I am very happy for you Karen. Good luck, and keep us posted on the rest of your news."

I assured him I would and the rest of the evening was taking care of patients with my feet inches off the floor. I felt as if I were walking on air.

Word spread throughout the operating room quickly and I was overwhelmed by the questions that were fired at me like a machine gun. The support I received from my co-workers was immeasurable. Oh, there were the skeptics and heretics who insisted I was mistaken or I must have been in the wrong, but I did not let the negatives deter my path ahead. I knew the truth, God knew the truth and I was going full steam ahead to get answers of a long delayed felony reconstruction. No stone was going to be unturned and no piece of information was going to be overlooked. I was much older and wiser now and no one was going to stand in my way of getting justice.

CHAPTER 21

COMMENCEMENT

I HAD RECEIVED TWO LETTERS FROM JAMIE since Sharon told him of our discovery. His first letter was shy, yet he seemed excited about the fact we were all found. His second letter was more informative about how we were going to remake our family and wanting to know where and how everyone was.

On Tuesday, July 29, 2003 at 1:15 pm, Lisa called me on my cell phone while I was driving from one hospital to the next and said, "Mom, you have to call in sick, I need you to help me."

"Why, what's up?"

"I can't tell you, but you need to call in sick now and meet me at my house." I could hear desperation in her voice.

"Lisa, you know I don't just call in sick if I am well, is there some sort of emergency. Are you sick, are the kids hurt?" My stomach was beginning to spasm and fear was creeping into my heart.

"We're going to get your son."

I hung up. I called my boss and told her what was happening and that I would not be in. She said she was happy for me and to be careful. I was back on the phone with Lisa in seconds.

"Ok, tell me what is going on."

"Jamie was released from jail early and I was supposed to pick him up here in Lakeland at the bus station. Then we were going to show up at your work and surprise you, but he missed his connection bus in Ocala when he walked across the street to the store. He asked me to come get him and then we would surprise you, but I want to surprise him with you, instead. He told me not to tell you, but you know I can't do that, I tell you everything, so are you coming?"

I arrived at Lisa's house at 1:45 pm and we were headed to Ocala five minutes later. The drive was the longest drive of my life, although it was only three hours. I was afraid I wouldn't recognize him or he wouldn't like me. I was afraid too much time had passed and I had no idea what he had been told. I knew I was being extremely sensitive and on edge as if a million mosquitoes were biting me, gnawing at my skin, but I was also excited beyond words and I could hardly sit still.

At exactly 4:23 pm, I saw him, the most beautiful sight my eyes had seen in a very long time. Jamie was standing outside the bus station smoking a cigarette and looking out into the parking lot. Lisa had no chance to park the truck; I jumped out and ran into his arms. I thought about that moment long after our meeting. My "little man" was a foot taller than I, and giggled—we must have been a sight! I held him so tight I am sure he was having difficulty breathing and we both just sobbed in each other's arms for what seemed to be an eternity. I was afraid to let go, and at that very moment, vowed *never* to let go again.

Next was Lisa's turn. Her big brother, her tormentor and teaser—the little guy who taught her to walk and slime kitchens, had returned. I was overwhelmed with joy as I watched brother and sister reconnect with a love so intense that I knew the moment had to be felt around the country. I knew my mother was smiling down on all of us and this was just the beginning. He met Allison, his niece who was six, and nephew, Christian, three years old and he quietly took it all in.

We began talking at sonic speed all the way home about him, his growing up, and school. I also found out that Allison was not my first grandchild. Jamie had a son who was eight years old and looked exactly like his father. We talked about all the things he wanted to do plus all the things we all wanted to do together.

When we arrived back in Lakeland, we met up with

his other sister, Gina. Another round of tears and hugs ensued and we all went to Beef O'Brady's for dinner and talked for hours. It was an exhausting day to say the least and he came home with me for the evening. He was supposed to go to Sharon and Franks when he was released as they had planned this little welcome home party for him. I know they were a bit disappointed that he chose to come "home" first but I promised them I would bring him to their place in Melbourne when we got up in the morning.

We sat up for hours talking and I know at times that he was unsure of all that I was saying. Not believing and wanting to believe everything in the same moment is a very confusing thing to do. I know the difficulty because I had experienced it for so many years. I told Jamie that we would pick up his sisters in the morning and take him to Melbourne, but we had another stop to make first. I slept soundly, I think for the first time in 23 years. My son, my only son, was asleep in the other room and all felt right with the world. I thanked God first for the miracle that had happened and then I thanked my Mom. "He can't climb into your arms right now, Mom, but I am sure that you don't mind!"

The next morning, we were off to pick up Lisa and Gina, but Gina had to work and couldn't come. Lisa and Jamie were talking wildly, each trying to catch up faster than the other, when I pulled into a construction site in Kissimmee. It was if radar was working in Ronnie's mind and in Jamie's mind because the truck became very silent. I was pulling up next to Ronnie's front-end loader and Jamie jumped out of the truck while it was still moving. Ronnie jumped off the loader, forgetting to put the bucket down, and grabbed his son. The moment will live on in my heart and mind forever as he proclaimed in tears, "My son, my son. I never thought I would see you again on this earth and God gave you back to me!" Tears flowed between both men and Ronnie just kept yelling to everyone around the job site, "This is my boy, my lost but found boy."

He was so proud and Jamie looked up at his daddy like he had never left. He looked like that six year old who adored his father every second of every day. I took pictures to capture the moment, but the pictures cannot begin to describe the raw, unbending love that was shared between father and son for the first time in so many wasted years.

We all went to lunch at Sonny's Bar-b-que and the conversation seemed to go on forever. He and his Dad were just yakking away as if they had never stopped and Ronnie said that he would be able to get him a job where he was working. Jamie was very excited about doing just that, working with his Dad.

After spending two hours at the restaurant, Ronnie had to get back to work. I had to get him home to Melbourne as promised where his "other" parents were waiting, then return to take care of the house and the usual routine. Life was getting better by the moment.

We arrived in Melbourne around 4:00 pm and I was reintroduced to Sharon and Frank. They genuinely loved him and were very happy to see him home. I knew that I had to leave him in their care, but leaving him was such an incredibly heart wrenching thing to do. He assured me that he wasn't going anywhere and he was a grown up now. No one could ever separate us again! I knew he was right, but I was still dealing with 23 years of loss for a six-year-old and was having great difficulty seeing him as a grown man, a grown man with grey hair! I was also very anxious to meet my "new" eight-year-old grandson, but was told that would have to wait. His mother was a difficult person to deal with and Jamie actually lived with his maternal grandparents.

On July 31, 2003, I met again with Mike and gave him the news about being with Jamie. He was thrilled because this meant we would have the "real" evidence the judge had requested. On September 3rd we learned the case had never been closed by the judge since 1986.

CHAPTER 22

CELEBRATION

I LOOKED FORWARD TO THE WEEKENDS with great joy in my heart because Jamie would come over. We would spend time learning about each other and what had been going on over the 23 years that had passed while we were apart. I knew he didn't trust me, since his information was easier to believe than mine. All he was told was I didn't want children and gave them up. He had no idea that his sisters grew up with me. Information that you have been absorbing for 23 years is much easier to accept and keep than information that is new or challenging. We had a long way to go, but we also had a long time to develop and grow.

With Jamie came information by the box load, but the most eye-opening piece of data that he told me about was his baby book. I had been telling him how I was sorry I didn't have it as each of the children had their own and it had been filled out with an enormous amount of detail about their infancy and beginning. He said, "Mom, I have my baby book. I have had it since I went to Sharon and Franks."

I was shocked, "You have it … I can't believe it."

I shared with him the story about how it disappeared from my existence so conveniently and he said, "Well, Mom, it isn't lost." This was one more item that triggered another angry moment from 23 years ago! He brought me his adoption papers, which we took straight to Mike. Our case took on new life, and with the hiring of a forensic specialist, a retired FBI agent; we proved that I did *not* sign any adoption papers.

Jamie told me he was never taken to the Boy's Ranch and that he was immediately taken to the Osceola Children's Home on Neptune Road. He said he was only there for a day and then went to Ms. D's house, the foster care mother. He doesn't remember how long, but remembered meeting Sharon and Frank in a group setting with other children playing at Ms. D's house. Shortly thereafter they became his new family and home. Hearing this from my son's own lips broke my heart into a million pieces. I didn't think I could hurt any more, as Frank had said, but I was wrong.

We discussed at great length the issue of his "death" and at first he just couldn't believe it. After a couple of weekends and further conversation, a memory was triggered. He recalled making a trip with his new parents to Kissimmee and stopping in St. Cloud right behind our "old" house when he was ten. He said he wandered over to the house and it was being renovated into a doctor's office. He remembered that an older lady used to live across the street from us who would pick our guavas to make jelly and bring us some every year. He walked over to see if she still lived there and she did. He asked her, "What happened to the people who lived across the street and do you know where they went?"

She told him, "Oh, they moved shortly after their little boy died, but I don't know where they moved to."

He said he looked at her sad face and replied, "That was me, I am their little boy and I am *not* dead." She was certainly surprised and deeply saddened again as she had no idea where we were or even where to look for us.

He went back across the street to the house and asked the workers if he could look inside as he used to live there. They let him and he said he remembered every inch of it, where his room was, his sisters room and our room. He said he remembered the Florida room and redoing the floor with his Dad.

Upon remembering all of this, Jamie became very sullen, realizing the horror of the truth and the extent they had gone to destroy a family. I assured him that no matter what HRS had done to us, it is now past and we can move forward by proving to them we can reconnect our family. We have a good attorney who is fighting for our rights and we will make them pay for what they have done to us. He agreed and we began planning his sisters' upcoming birthdays.

I was so overjoyed with the return of my son and I wanted to introduce him to the world, again! Lisa, Gina, and I decided to throw him a Welcome Home party. Jamie was thinking that we were planning the party was for his sisters' birthdays since Gina's was August 15th and Lisa's was August 27th. It was sort of difficult the keep the three of them from figuring it all out, but with the help of my girlfriend, Denys, we managed to get it all together. The party was scheduled for August 16, 2003 and many people were invited. We invited my co-workers, close friends both from the area and church, along with the entire family. The cake that we ordered was a full sheet cake and it said, "*Welcome home Jamie*" on top and underneath at each corner was "*Happy Birthday Lisa*" and, "*Happy Birthday Gina.*" Denys did a fantastic job of keeping it hidden until the main event.

Everyone ate great food and welcomed Jamie home. Everyone instantly loved him, as I knew they would, with his electric, charismatic personality. He was still the life of the party as he had been when he was six and had everyone mesmerized with his stories. He was, however, surprised since he thought that the party was for Lisa and Gina, and he made it known to me that he had even brought them presents.

The party started winding down and my children, Denys, and I went into the house. Jamie presented his sisters with their presents. Gina opened hers first and it was a baby doll with a card for a three year old. Lisa's was also a baby doll and a card for a four year old. It was so endearing because he said, "Think about it, Mom, it is really their next birthday to me since I left, and this should be their third and fourth birthdays. So, I have brought them gifts appropriate to those ages." We all laughed at the sincerity and thoughtfulness, then we cried that he missed those days and all the birthdays that followed. It was group hug time and all felt so right with the world. At least for the moment!

Jamie and I have had many ups and down, mostly related to the information he received and information he believed, if only in his mind. The mind of a six-year-old little boy was harmed and his entire life was disrupted and changed forever because some horribly sadistic person had no regard for life or family.

CHAPTER 23

EVIDENCE

ON SEPTEMBER 13, 2003, I was getting ready to leave for a trip up North and Jamie and Lisa called me to say we have to have a talk. It was serious and it couldn't wait. I told them we could plan on meeting as soon as I got back, but both insisted that it should be now. We agreed to meet at the Olive Garden in North Lakeland and have lunch. I was so happy to see them together, kind of hanging out sister and brother, but neither of them looked happy. Before the food came, Jamie handed me an envelope and Lisa said to me, "Mom, why didn't you tell me Daddy wasn't my father?"

"*What?*" Ah hah, Pandora's Box is beginning to show itself. "What on earth are you talking about?"

Jamie pointed to the envelope I held in my hands

and said it was in there. The food arrived and we said the blessing over the food and I thanked God for this precious moment I and asked that He straighten all of this confusion out. The two of them began to eat and I began to read. It was an interview allegedly between some members of H.R.S. and me. I could not believe what I was reading—lies, disgusting lies, so horrific I became physically ill. They had the audacity to put in ink a disgusting thing about my mother and how her boyfriend at the time was my daughter, Lisa's, biological father. I completely lost my appetite and asked Jamie if I could have it. He told me he didn't need it or want it, so I planned to take it directly to Mike's office when we were finished with lunch. I was already finished with lunch and hadn't even touched it. The waitress asked me if I would like to take it with me and I just stated, "I won't eat it, but thank you anyway."

I assured my children that the paper I held in my hands contained mostly fabricated lies and that I knew who the father of all my children was. They had taken some of the information from our counseling sessions long ago and mixed them up into something they could use to justify stealing my son. Then Jamie proceeded to tell me he had been told a long time ago that Lisa did indeed have another father than the one she believed. I called her father so they could talk and they decided the easiest and most definitive way to solve all of this was to have DNA tests done. Ronnie assured Lisa that he indeed was her father and that no one else could claim her. They arranged to meet the next day and find out what they would have to do to acquire the testing materials or where they could have it done. It was just another item on the list of things those disgusting people came up with. Jamie was upset and didn't know what to think about any of it, as he had heard these lies for a long time. Now all that he thought he knew was being disputed. Ronnie and I were intent on proving to him that we were not now, nor had we ever, lied to him about anything.

Directly after leaving the restaurant, I walked into Mike's office with the garbage I held in my hand. I was trembling, red faced, and tearful which made it difficult for me to talk. He told me to take my time and regroup if I needed to. He had a few moments and no appointments at that time. I recomposed myself, informing him how I came to have the information I was holding, and told him it was a nasty compilation of information given during many counseling sessions. No interview of any kind had ever taken place with any of the people listed and I was now dealing with the pain they caused my daughter so she would believe that I had lied to her about her parentage. I would contact him upon my return to Florida and I hoped that more hateful, hurtful information did not come to light while I was gone. He told me to take a copy of this, which he copied for me, and pick it apart paragraph by paragraph. I started the process on the plane and continued through my entire time up North.

In October, Lisa and her Dad contacted a genetic facility and ordered the items that they needed to complete the tests. She and her Dad met at his house with his girlfriend as a witness and did the necessary swabs, two from his cheek and two from hers. They placed all the information into sealed envelopes and mailed them on to the lab in California. Lisa wanted desperately to believe the things we were telling her, but until the DNA returned, she was depressed and confused. No matter how many times we told her that Ronnie was her father, it would have to be proven to her and that in itself was both saddening and upsetting to her father, her, and myself. She had never questioned us before, and now not only did Jamie doubt things about us, she doubted also. After they went to the post office, they called me and said, "It is in the mail, we have to wait about six to eight weeks before we know anything." I told Lisa, there was no doubt in my mind that her Daddy was Ronnie and this test would prove it. She just said to me, "I hope so, Mom."

The holidays came and it was complete for me in many ways. Jamie was there with my grandson and a couple of times he would start saying something with the word, "Mommy." I would just laugh and it would feel so right that my heart swelled three times over. Looking at Jamie Junior was indeed a bit odd for me because he is a carbon copy of his father, right down to mannerisms, and I was getting things mixed up in my mind about which was my son and who was my grandchild. He had the same dark mahogany color hair, cocoa colored eyes with long thick lashes that would, like his father's, capture the eye of any female wishing they had such a beautiful attribute. Thank God, after Christmas, I could run to Trudy, my counselor, and have her help me with a lot of it. I was confused about so much and angry about more.

February 12, 2004 at approximately 11:45 in the morning, I received a call from Lisa screaming in my ear, "Mommy, Daddy is my Daddy, *he is* my Daddy!"

I knew this is how it would turn out and said, "Honey, I told you he was, now call him as he has probably gotten the paper too, but he is at work now and I know he would love to hear you say that to him." She hung up and did just that. Lisa was again walking around with a smile on her face and walking tall.

Jamie told her, "You know Mom is a nurse and she could have changed the results." But Lisa told him, "Mom had nothing to do with this and I am sure she doesn't know anyone in California at that institute to change anything. Jamie, she doesn't have that kind of pull!"

He finally accepted the fact that we were at least not lying about that.

CHAPTER **24**

MOMENTUM

MIKE TOLD ME TO GO to the St. Cloud Police Department and file a kidnapping charge after yet another decline from the judge, which I did. I called them at 8:00 in the morning on March 3rd, 2004. Lisa and I drove over there after speaking to a detective on the phone. It seemed so odd to be sitting there with police officers, Officer S and Officer M, after all that had happened, but I knew it was the right thing to do. They indeed did kidnap my son, and then either sold him or, for whatever other reason, gave him to people to adopt. The answer to that, I may never know.

At 12:25 in the afternoon, I filled out and signed a sworn statement after writing the events down on a piece of paper. I had written on another piece of paper the names of my family members and witnesses for them to use that would substantiate my claim. We left shortly after that and they told me that Officer M. would investigate it and get back to me.

Approximately May 7th, Officer M. called me and told me that they wanted to do their own forensic examination of my signature. I told them that I had no problem with that until she told me exactly what it was they wanted me to do. I was to go into their office and sign thirty copies of the original surrender papers for them to examine my signature. I am sure that anyone with any sanity certainly would have difficulty doing such a thing. I was not in favor of that move, especially since I had NOT signed the original one.

After all that I had experienced including the fraud I had lived through, the idea of them substituting one of these for the original seemed to be a frightening possibility. I am well aware of the advanced technology of computers in this day and age and I wasn't about to do that so they could somehow electronically exchange one for the other, however, the Officer could not understand my hesitation. She claimed that since I was sitting in the Police Department where I was safe, nothing like that could happen, and I laughed. I wasn't sure if it was by her own naive understanding of police duty, lack of common sense, or maybe even stupidity, but to say that "Nothing like that could happen," was just too much for me.

You have to understand, I trust absolutely no one in

the government that has anything to do with my children or my family. She informed me that the forms were going to be reviewed by the Orlando U.S. Secret Service (wow, I now felt really important) and be examined by Special Agent J. G. and that was their request for the signatures. The other specialist that examined and stated I did not sign the document, wanted evidence of my signature back in 1980. I asked the attorney about it and he said to go ahead and make sure that my daughter was sitting there with me, once again, and witnessed me signing these papers as the officer numbered the back of each one. This way, I was complying to facilitate the investigation and they could get things completed. Detective M. stated she would be in touch with me.

I called the police department on June 8th to see if they had reached any conclusion yet and she told me very directly, "no." I would be receiving the report in the mail when it was complete.

On June 24th of 2004, I received her investigative report. Typed clearly and in bold letters on the front, it read, "Unfounded for the case of Kidnapping." I could not believe my eyes and, when I read the report, it angered me even more. I took this over to Mike and he shook his head. Again, I needed to dispute this information because it appeared the only people interviewed regarding the entire event were from the Department of Health and Rehabilitative Services. The report was full of discrepancies and was misleading to anyone that would read it. I feel that the investigator was extremely biased to say the least. All she managed to extract was untrue information, all of which made me appear to be a monster.

This particular investigator stated she had been given the case for investigation on April 16, 2004, but I was in there talking to her and another deputy on March 3, 2004. I wondered why there was such a delay, six and a half weeks to be exact, after writing my sworn statement in front of both of them. Six days later, she claimed she went to the Orlando Administrative Offices to interview a woman apparently in a managerial capacity at the present time. She brought forth documents of menial value, in my mind, as she could only produce the bogus interview with myself and some people that were never around me from Osceola County, a "Surrender of Custody" paper that allegedly I signed, and by her own words, she was "unable to provide adoption papers since it had been such a long time since the adoption."

I pondered that statement for a long while and thought, how convenient they would keep some legal documents, yet not others, in a government office. I found that very strange, but then again I have been dealing with this entity of the government for 23 years now, and wondered why the detective didn't ask why the file was not complete. However, I feel she wasn't really looking for the truth. This Ms. N also had in her possession a letter that I supposedly wrote to Jamie that was supposed to be attached to the copy of our investigative report, however, it was not. This letter, in the report, claims that on January 12, 1981, I called Ms. B in the Osceola office and told her I had written a letter to my son that he could read when he was 18 years old. Some of the contents of the letter are included in the investigative report, and just those small excerpts that I read sounded as if a psychological counselor had written them, not a desperate 24-year-old mother who was trying to have her child returned to her.

The letter states that I brought it to the office on February 25, 1981, which of course, is six weeks later than the phone call. Not to mention it was also 11 days after Ronnie and I sat at the Ranch for over three hours waiting to see Jamie with Valentine presents and a card. That is the time we were told that Jamie could not return to an abusive family and he had been moved.

The most bizarre thing that horrified me was the next statement. I read it over and over again as I perused the report, yet it didn't sink into my conscious mind until six years after receiving it. Here is what I read: "On 02/25/81, Ms. B. received the letter and placed it in Jamie's baby book." The same baby book that had mysteriously disappeared after the copy machine had broken, and was never returned to me. February 25, 1981 was five months after they had taken Jamie and claimed to have lost his baby book. I almost fainted while writing this book because my conscious mind actually grasped everything while doing my research. I had missed this one so very important statement too many times. It was proof that they did indeed have the baby book they claimed they had lost.

The report also states that the detective called DCF in Kissimmee and spoke to a Ms. R who claimed to be the investigator at the time. She goes on to detail fabricated lies about how I was determined to leave my child at the office and that I did indeed leave him there. If you will recall, he was picked up from my house two days after I agreed for him to have the testing. The agency investigator during that time was someone other than Ms. R. I know this because I spoke with the person many times trying to see my son and her name was Ms. H. I will never forget her name, because she was a constant contact for me during that time. It confirms my belief that the people who worked for the HRS department would say anything to cover up their own nasty deeds.

Then, to add insult to injury, came blatant lies from the foster care mother who actually had the audacity to tell the detective that I had met her, and that she was in a hallway watching me with the workers as I openly gave up my son. She stated that I visited Jamie at her house in order to have a birthday party for his sister. Of course, we would not dream of having the party at our own house, especially for his sister. Her unfamiliar house would be the best place. What is even more preposterous is that she told the detective she brought Jamie to the HRS office in order to be picked up for a visit for the day! She claimed she could not remember if I dropped him off at the HRS office or her residence. The foster mother, Ms. D, went on to say the most hurtful thing about me considering she truly had *never* met me or ever laid eyes on me, "Ms. Marshall seemed to be cold hearted and determined to give her child up for adoption. Jamie couldn't understand why his mother had left him. Jamie had tried his best to be good in order to go back with his mother one day." I am sure that God in Heaven was recording the moment she gave a completed and sworn written statement of lies.

No one from my family, not one person that lived in that area, nor any friends of mine, was ever interviewed. Not one question was asked of them! She did not ask my Priest, she did not interview their pediatrician; she did not interview my in-laws, or his teachers in school. She simply asked *no one* any questions about me, our family, or circumstances other than HRS individuals. That is what I call the most incompetent investigation of all time. The forensic investigation from their Secret Services evaluation stated, "There are some indications that Karen may have executed the signature on the questioned document, but the evidence is far from conclusive."

In other words according to many attorneys and mine, it isn't my signature, but since they are both government entities, they don't want to be heard going against the department of HRS and state that I did *not* sign the document.

The agency made another *huge* mistake. They forgot to get rid of the one paper I actually did sign; the "Parents Consent for Foster Home Placement and Medical Care." This paper states that Jamie will be in their custody for a short period of time and the signature was required in the event he needed medical attention. It states, "I consent to such transportation, medical care and treatment as the Department may consider necessary for the health and welfare of my child. I agree for my child to be given periodic health examinations, tests, immunizing treatments, and hospitalization if needed. In the event of any serious illness or accident, I understand that the Department agrees to make every possible effort to communicate with me immediately, but if it is impossible to locate me, I want the Department to authorize whatever medical care, including surgery, is necessary for the health of my child. I agree to assume financial responsibility to the extent of my ability to pay in accordance with a separate financial agreement."

This document was signed September 8, 1980 and was never witnessed or notarized at that time. It was however notarized officially on October 1, 1985, two weeks after I filed to have my son's adoption file opened to find his grave! If I had intended to give up all rights to my son, I would not have signed this form. I would have indeed signed the surrender papers they forged!

CHAPTER **25**

UNSETTLED

MIKE WAS A CONSTANT CHAMPION as he encountered block after block regarding our case. He never lost hope. If he did, he never let me know it either by his manor or his words. He said, "Karen, because of the civil aspect of this case, we need to hire board certified civil trial lawyers as it is beyond the realm of my practice. We are in need of attorneys that have the expertise and are not afraid to go against the "system," the system being Health and Rehabilitative Services, now known as the Department of Children and Families." I told him I will do whatever he thinks is best as long as he is standing by my side, because he is the only person I trusted after having learned over the years to trust no one.

On June 23, 2004, we hired our first set of civil trial lawyers, P&M. Excitement was escalating as we all walked out of their office thinking those responsible are finally going to be confronted by the law and pay for their criminal involvement in stealing my little boy. We are going to be vindicated at last and I wanted to look into the faces of those horrible people and let them know that they could not then, nor now, deter the path of God by destroying a family, my family! God brought us all back together and no one else was going to ever separate us again. We sort of became one big extended family with Sharon, Frank, and all of us. Unfortunately one of the partners in their firm had a critical accident, which left the other partner with an enormous case load. He regretfully resigned from our case November 3, 2004.

This would not deter us or Mike and we were back on the crusade to find another firm. On December 3, 2004, we signed with KVM and for whatever reason, probably fear of the "System", yet again, they resigned and referred us to KG on April 23, 2004.

On May 4, 2004, KG actually submitted a "Notice of Intent" to the Department of Children and Families. Jamie, Lisa, Gina and I were again thinking the end was near and that we were finally going to get somewhere. She discovered, among other things, that there had never been any type of investigation of me regarding child abuse. There was not one mention that I was harming my child or children, and no record anywhere of any type of action. This was their very big mistake, as they had no recourse for taking my son.

However, that was not to be! On March 23, 2005, the KG attorney also quit. My depression was creeping up into the well of my heart and I was beginning to think that again, there was no one that could take on the magnitude of this adventure. We were all bonding beautifully as a family, all believing that the light at the end of the tunnel was getting brighter, only for the tunnel to close up tight again. How in the world can this keep happening? We were just beside ourselves and even Ronnie was thinking that this was a conspiracy or some sort of treachery going on, as they wanted to protect their own, no matter what evil things they had done. The evil was going to prevail and after each time of getting so close, we were sent back another mile. It was not fair, but we were *not* going to give up, not after all the setbacks and heartaches for so long.

I was discussing the predicament with the doctors, surgeons, managers, and staff at my hospital and they all, almost unanimously said, "Take it to the press, that could stir up the worms and maybe some attorney out there will find this case too interesting to pass up." "Call the major Networks, newspapers and go for Public Awareness, get the public outcry … you know what happens when the 'people' are involved. Things get done!" They were right, that is what we had to do, get the public involved and see what came out of the woodwork.

I got started and called NBC Dateline, 48 Hours, The Lakeland Ledger and many local news stations. I even spoke with several others as well, to no avail. When I finally did get responses, they all wanted it to be in trial, not at the stage we were at now. I was getting close to the end of my rope, when I found one lonely reporter who wanted to print my story, only to have the court say we couldn't use names and we had to have an outcome already established.

We are *not* done yet! We will never give up this fight. We *will* find someone who has the guts and tenacity to take on the Department of Health and Rehabilitative Services, get to the heart of this matter and make them answer for all they have done. I have endured the pain of this "crime" for far too long, as well as my family. We will prevail and we will win!

My best friend Misty, who was there at the start of these adventures in my life since 1974 and succumbed to pancreatic cancer in February of 2007, told me to never give up. My beloved Ronnie, husband, best friend, and father of my children succumbed to lung cancer in June of 2008, also said to me, "Never let the Bastards get away with this, baby, he is our boy and they deserve to get what is coming to them!" My family has been through enough but we will continue the fight.

I remember watching an interview with John Walsh on December 16, 2008, televised on MSNBC. Walsh's son, Adam, had been murdered on July 27, 1981, just

2 months and 12 days after my son died. I related with his awful pain. I listened to this man's anguish 27 years later as he stated regarding missing children: "Justice delayed is not justice denied. To all those who haven't received justice, don't give up hope. To all parents of missing children, murdered children, and crime victims, the criminal justice system is sometimes the criminal in the justice system. Don't give up hope. Sometimes you have to stay in there by yourself. Sometimes you're the best and last hope to get justice for yourself."

I will never give up hope in receiving justice for what this agency did to my family.

EPILOG

THE DEPARTMENT OF CHILDREN and Families or Health and Rehabilitative Services is a system that is terribly broken. They have managed to be in the press numerous times for unthinkable acts, including:

"Group claims HRS kidnaps kids, tramples rights. Most child abuse claims are unfounded, and many children removed from homes by HRS investigators are abused in state foster homes. These children do not come back the same way as when they left. They are deeply scarred."

- 1988 IN THE ORLANDO SENTINEL

"On Wednesday, June 7, 2000, a $501 million dollar civil class action suit was filed and accepted on behalf of families who allegedly have been victimized by the practices of DCF and Juvenile courts. The suit alleges that the state engaged in

a systematic process by which the families, parents, children, and citizens of the State have been terrorized, traumatized, and torn asunder as well as deprived of their fundamental rights without due process of law."

- June 16, 2000
United States District Court, Florida

Governor Bush:

"State needs new approach for finding missing children. The South Florida Sun-Sentinel easily found several children who became missing while in the custody of the Department of Children & Families. In April, the child welfare agency acknowledged losing 5-year-old Rilya Wilson. The little girl had been missing since January 2001 and no caseworker had checked on her for 15 months."

- Tuesday, August 13, 2002

The state's child abuse hot line got a worried call in May 2008, alleging that a baby's father had passed out snorting cocaine and the boy was chewing on a wire. Jarkevis Allen's father rejected an offer for drug treatment and the case was closed within the required 60 days. Five months later, 1 year old Jarkevis was dead.

- Saturday, February 13, 2010

LeHigh Acres Florida:

Three child welfare workers were fired Friday over the handling of a case involving a 13 year-old girl who was found raped and fatally beaten while in state care. The immediate supervisor on her case, a 23-year veteran with DCF, was fired for negligence and misconduct along with two others in charge of her care.

- June 24, 2006

Orlando Sentinel:

"Child Abuse means big bucks for the government."
"Taking a child out of a home can be worth $45,000.00 per year for a normal kid and $90,000.00 per year for a "special needs" child."

- Statistics in 2006

Lastly in the news:

"Child Welfare workers in Daytona Beach area failed to ensure that criminal background checks were performed on child care workers. Preliminary investigations by the DCF showed that more than 100 child care centers may not have had the proper screenings and inspections because of problems with two DCF workers. Authorities say it appears that some reports may have been forged. One of the workers was fired and the other resigned. Falsifying DCF records is a felony, but the two have not been charged."

- Associated Press
Miami Herald, July 19, 2010

GET THE PICTURE? If the agency gets a foster family to care for a child, then pays the family pittance per child per day, there is more money left over to take more kids.

The list is endless and they are getting away with murder. I hope reading this book has enlightened you to take charge of your life as I said in the beginning. Take charge of your family and of those who are too insecure or small to do it for themselves. I am fully aware of what the Department of Health and Rehabilitative Services has done to my family. Not a day goes by that I don't feel the pain and sorrow for believing in a system that does not work. I paid the price with my son, our family, and none of us will ever be the same. I allowed them into our family, thinking that their counseling center would help me be a better mother and teach me to deal with a normal six-year-old boy, who I was told wasn't normal. I will forever feel guilty for thinking I was doing the right thing.

GOD BLESS YOU AND HOPEFULLY YOU ARE NOW AN AWARE PUBLIC!

"But whosoever shall offend one of these little ones which believe in me, it would be better for him to have a great millstone hanged about his neck, and to be drowned in the depths of the sea".

- Matt 18:6